THE
ENDANGERED
CUSTOMER

Also by Richard R. Shapiro

The Welcomer Edge: Unlocking the Secrets to Repeat Business

THE
ENDANGERED
CUSTOMER

8 STEPS TO GUARANTEE REPEAT BUSINESS

RICHARD R. SHAPIRO

THE CENTER FOR CLIENT RETENTION
BERKELEY HEIGHTS, NJ

Published by
The Center For Client Retention
Berkeley Heights, NJ

Publisher's Cataloging-in-Publication Data
Shapiro, Richard R.

The endangered customer : 8 steps to guarantee repeat business / Richard R. Shapiro. – Berkeley Heights, NJ : The Center For Client Retention, 2016.

p. ; cm.

ISBN13: 978-0-9980030-0-9

1. Customer services. 2. Consumer satisfaction. 3. Relationship marketing. I. Title.

HF5415.5.S534 2016
658.812—dc23   2015953553

FIRST EDITION, second printing

Project coordination by Jenkins Group, Inc.
www.BookPublishing.com

Interior design by Brooke Camfield

Printed in the United States of America
22   21   20   19   18   •   6   5   4   3   2

To my Dad who taught me,

Customers are people first,
customers second.

Generating repeat business is easy.
It's all about creating and building relationships.

Contents

Introduction

If any part of your business enterprise relies on your relationship with consumers, beware of the "Age of Endangerment." At no point in history has your customer base been more vulnerable to poaching than it is today. A recent global consumer study by Accenture states that an ongoing steady erosion in customer loyalty is "one of the most compelling findings of our research." In a digital, self-reliant era, choices and competition are immediately accessible on a 24-hour basis, serving what Accenture terms the new "nonstop consumer." Today's consumers have more choices and are better informed and more likely to switch to competing providers than ever before. The result is a global "Switching Economy" that Accenture estimates is worth $6.2 trillion—revenues lost for some companies and gained for others.[1]

The Switching Economy is growing fast—up 26 percent in just four years.[2] Now the challenge every company faces is how to stifle this ominous consumer trend. How can you prevent the loss of your endangered customers while capturing new customers? There will be winners and losers in the $6.2-trillion annual contest for the endangered customer. This book provides a battle plan for winning.

I have spent my entire working life in the customer service industry and 28 years ago created The Center For Client Retention (TCFCR) to address this growing problem with Fortune 500 companies. The lesson learned from my experience is that companies, of any size and in any consumer channel, can survive and thrive in the Switching Economy by making human connections that build sustainable customer relationships even in the consumer-driven demand chain, where every customer knows best. In order to generate repeat business and avoid customer attrition, companies must constantly create customer experiences that nurture positive, personalized, and human connectivity on the web, in the store, or with a mobile device. Quite a paradox indeed!

The goal of this book is to offer a road map for continuously creating emotional bonds that generate the very highest levels of customer loyalty. My hope is that readers will come to see that it is still possible to create extreme customer loyalty in a highly threatening consumer ecosystem. By the time you've finished the last chapter, you should be asking yourself the same question in every service delivery discussion and at every staff meeting: "Where is the human connection?"

Research shows ample evidence of how losing companies are failing in the battle for the endangered customer. Too many companies are reactive only in their customer relationships and often fail to deliver a prompt resolution of service problems they create. A 2014 American Express study found that 61 percent of customers say they have switched to a competitor due to bad service.[3] Accenture's studies echo this finding. Fifty-three percent of US consumers told Accenture that bad service prompted them to switch to a competing company, but *80 percent* of these switches would have been avoided if the poor service had been met with prompt resolution.[4] Poor service followed by more poor service—that's how you endanger your customers into becoming someone else's customers.

When Accenture researched the specific customer service failures consumers find very frustrating,[5] these familiar six situations ranked at the very top of the list:

1. Having to contact the company multiple times for the same reason.

2. Being on hold for a long time when contacting the company.

3. Having to repeat the same information to multiple employees of the company or through multiple channels.

4. Dealing with employees or self-help sites/systems that cannot answer my questions.

5. Having a company deliver something different from what it promises up front.

6. Dealing with employees who are unfriendly or impolite.

In my own informal poll of customer pet peeves, I heard:

1. You watch people cutting into the line and the business does nothing to prevent it.

2. You find out that the person next to you on the plane paid $200 less than you for the same flight.

3. You unsubscribe to an online site that continues to e-mail you twice a day . . . forever.

4. An appliance or tech accessory fails one week past its warranty expiration date and the company refuses to honor the warranty without so much as a sincere apology.

5. You try to get a new license or other government document and you need to visit five service windows to complete the transaction.

6. Your cell number is entered in the National Do Not Call Registry and you still get annoying sales calls.

7. The restaurant automatically adds a 20 percent gratuity for fair to crummy service.

8. You are waiting in a long line for the only open bank teller window and five other tellers and bank managers are busy doing paperwork in the background.

9. Your dry cleaner insists that the spot on your new outfit was already there.

10. The waiter takes away your plate before others in your party are finished.

All of these frustrations share one vital common thread. Each one represents a customer touch point in which the business has broken its "human connection" with the customer. These slights and irritations, which can seem rather minor when described in isolation, create negative feelings that are hard for customers to shake. And in the Switching Economy, where "nonstop consumers" have no shortage of alternative choices, the quickest and most natural balm for hurt feelings is to make a switch to a competitor. The lifetime value of a customer can be lost in one fumbled interaction. This is why today, in the words of Jack Mitchell, chairman of Mitchell Family Stores, "it's more important to know your customers than your merchandise."

In my first book, *The Welcomer Edge: Unlocking the Secrets to Repeat Business*, I described a simple three-step model for making a human connection with each and every customer interaction: the greet, the assist, and the leave-behind. You begin by welcoming each customer into your place of business as you would welcome that customer into your home. Then you engage the customer in conversation, in order to know the customer as a person first before discussing what that person needs as a customer. And, finally, upon each customer's departure, you invite that person to return by expressing a sincere wish to see him or her again. These are the frontline fundamentals to starting and maintaining the human connection.

I think the customer journey should be one that starts and never ends. Jon Stewart, on his final show, spoke elegantly and summed it up: "An artist I really admire once said that he thinks of his career as a long conversation with the audience, a dialogue. Nothing ends; it's a pause in the conversation. So rather than saying good-bye or goodnight, I'm just going to say I'm going to get a drink. And I'm sure I'll see you guys before I leave." So, too, with the customer experience; it is like a long conversation with some pauses but should always be resumed.

In *The Endangered Customer* expanded model, there are eight crucial stages in every customer's journey, from the moment he or she encounters your place of business (in person, by phone, or online) to the time following the purchase, when customer loyalty is put to the test. Each of the following eight chapters corresponds to one stage in that customer journey.

Chapter 1, "Make Me Feel Welcome," explores the ways companies should make each customer feel wanted and appreciated from the first encounter. Chapter 2, "Give Me Your Full Attention," discusses the challenges of providing appropriate attention to customers in an age characterized by distraction. "Answer More Than My Question," chapter 3, takes a deep look at the customer's desire for care and responsiveness in the shopping experience.

The next two chapters address the customer's need for your active involvement in the shopping experience. Chapter 4, "Know Your Stuff," emphasizes the extreme importance of giving your staff access to the knowledge necessary to satisfy the ever-growing information demands of today's customers. Chapter 5, "Don't Tell Me No," shows how to avoid the damaging effects of indifferent or inadequate responses to customer inquiries.

The final three chapters of the book reflect the most commonly ignored portion of the customer journey—what happens after money changes hands. Chapter 6, "Invite Me to Return," explores a common-sense step in building customer loyalty that is very often overlooked. Chapter 7, "Show Me I Matter," discusses the many ways to make gestures of customer appreciation that remind customers of their importance to you. The final chapter, "Surprise Me in Good Ways," takes a look at the significance of surprise throughout the customer journey and its particular value in generating loyalty among your very best customers.

All eight of these principles can be universally applied because the essential ingredients to build loyalty are no different from one sales channel to the next. The e-commerce sites that we return to again and again are the ones that offer us the same feeling of being valued that we get from the best, most service-oriented brick-and-mortar stores.

At the end of each chapter you will find a recap with power points that can be implemented by any organization. Most are "low-hanging fruit" and virtually cost free. Others require technology, staffing, or training and development. In order to prevent your loyal customers from becoming someone else's, additional investment in customer experience is inevitable, and accountability for results should start at the top. Salesforce CEO Marc Benioff has gone so far as to say that in this new era, "the CEO is now in charge of the customer relationship."

After the final chapter, you will find the Repeat Business Scorecard that's been created by TCFCR based on its 28 years of research. There are two survey questions for each of the eight customer journey stages described in the book. These 16 questions in total, when included as a part of your ongoing customer survey processes, will establish a baseline for your performance and help determine which action items require your immediate attention or offer opportunities to further leverage your company's strengths.

Improving your company's performance in all eight of these customer journey stages will generate levels of customer loyalty that you have never seen before. The eight steps are also designed to complement all the customer experience work you are already doing. By utilizing the principles behind each of the stages, you can better assess the effectiveness of your current customer experience initiatives.

If you manage to improve your performance in all eight of these areas, you will discover, to quote Aristotle's maxim, that the whole is much greater than the sum of its parts. On the other hand, if you neglect any one of these areas, you might be endangering your customer base. Inattention to any one of these eight phases drains your company's effectiveness in executing on the other seven. It's critical to *inspect what you expect*, allowing your organization to determine its strengths, opportunities, and shortcomings to help your associates focus on those priorities that will positively impact your percentage of repeat patrons. The recommended survey questions will help accomplish this goal.

Ultimately, your entire organization must fully recognize the importance of investing in customer loyalty because the digital age has made it so fragile. Today, for many enterprises, the connection between customer experience and profits is finally becoming clear. Analysis by Forrester Research showed that 10-year investment returns from public companies ranked at the top of Forrester's Customer Experience Index outperformed the S&P 500 by a sizeable margin, while consumer experience laggards on the Forrester index generated negative returns.[6]

I know firsthand how easily a company's management imperatives and short-term financial goals can undermine customer service while taking customer loyalty for granted. Although my first lessons about customer loyalty were learned as a teenager in my dad's men's clothing store (where customer loyalty was valued above everything else), I experienced the other side of the coin years later, while working for a Fortune 500 company.

At this particular company, cost cutting was uniformly applauded as a very good thing. General managers for each of the 40 regions were rewarded with large bonuses and lavish vacation trips if they exceeded their monthly goals in revenue and profits. To achieve those objectives and win the bonuses, managers found that the most tempting area for "improved efficiencies" was in the customer service budget.

Over time, I learned that service cutbacks proved to be a very reliable leading indicator of high customer turnover. The pattern became predictable. Regions that reported the highest profitability in one quarter would inevitably show a rise in customer churn rate and a drop in customer satisfaction survey scores during the following quarter. Within a year, that region would fall into the lower ranks of profitability. The customers who were responsible for making the region a winner for that one quarter felt so ill served that within a year, many of them had moved on to our competitors.

Customers are very quick to catch on to a company that is saving money at their expense. As important as it is to work within your budget, the temptation to boost short-term profits by cutting customer service needs to be acknowledged and addressed. New customers are very difficult and very expensive to find, as any sales and marketing professional will tell you. Retaining the customers you already have by treating them well is a great deal easier and more cost-effective than searching for new ones. It also happens to be more fun and personally fulfilling.

Preparing for the future

Sitting on our dining room table, about the size of two stacked soup cans, is a black cylindrical device that answers to the name of Alexa. It is the Amazon Echo, an always-on, always-listening device that responds to our every whim. Alexa provides us with music, sports scores, weather, and other information, whenever we ask. It's an artificial intelligence device, and because she's connected to Amazon's cloud servers, Alexa keeps getting smarter.

Alexa; her Apple counterpart, Siri; and Google Voice all represent what I consider to be the greatest threat imaginable to any consumer business. Soon, while watching TV, you'll be able to idly ask for a price on the best available TV with a larger screen. Alexa, Siri, or Google Voice will send you your new TV without a second thought. With Alexa, you won't even need to touch your mobile phone.

Consumer expectations for these forms of ease and convenience are escalating at a geometric rate. No one knows this better than Amazon CEO Jeff Bezos, who might be considered Alexa's father. "It's our job every day to make every important aspect of the customer experience a bit better," Bezos has said. He pushes his people to keep expanding the boundaries of what makes an exceptional customer experience.

"We watch our competitors, learn from them, see the things that they were doing for customers, and copy those things as much as we can." Bezos knows that e-commerce makes it easier than ever to lose customers if they feel ill served or mistreated, so he emphasizes the importance of making an emotional connection, even if it's through artificial intelligence. "We see our customers as invited guests to a party," Bezos says, "and we are the hosts."[7]

Companies can no longer succeed by differentiating themselves along the age-old standards of price, quality, and service. New developments on the horizon are poised to wipe those differentiators away. Disruptive start-ups are undercutting established firms on pricing because the nature of their funding doesn't require them to turn a short-term profit. The global economy continues to level the playing field on the matter of quality. And prompt, efficient service is now the gold standard and new differentiator, particularly among the rising Millennial Generation. College debt and changes in the economy indicate that Millennials as a group have less disposable income than their parents had at the same age, so they tend to be price-conscious shoppers. But studies show they are also willing to pay a little more for better service and are willing to spend more with companies that are socially responsible.[8]

All these changes suggest that the value created through making human connections will continue to grow in magnitude. Advances in shopping technology make it virtually impossible to predict what the future of customer experience will look like. What is certain, however, is that the human spirit can't be separated from human transactions and interactions—nor should it be. Customers do not want their lives filled with endless robotic encounters. As automated transactions become faster, easier, and more reliable, making the human connection will become increasingly rare—and therefore increasingly more valuable.

Those companies that will continue to deliver personalized service will create and sustain relationships that will positively impact bottom-line revenues and profitability. Organizations can meet these new challenges by employing technology that can be used to enhance, not diminish, the relationship. Hiring the right people and training them to recognize the customer as a person first will give your company a tremendous advantage. Equally important is keeping associates who know your customers. Employee appreciation and acknowledgment are just as consequential as focusing on great customer service. Paying employees to stay will truly nurture long-term customer relationships and produce significant dividends for any business.

The interesting paradox is the necessity to deploy technology in an environment in which the human-to-human touch will create a winning strategy. As automated transactions become faster, easier, and more reliable, only those companies that can deliver personalized service will be able to create and build loyal, lasting relationships to boost revenues and profitability over the long term. The big takeaway is that the human factor remains the primary determining force in the choices consumers make. We already said, and it bears repeating, that as human connections become increasingly rare, they also become increasingly valuable. The greatest differentiator for any company will be how well it makes that human connection with its endangered customers.

1

Make Me Feel Welcome

One day a few years ago, my wife and I went into a charming North Carolina antique store where we were greeted with a sign that read, "Come in as Strangers, Leave as Friends." When I saw the sign, I smiled and thought that's what every company's goal should be. To earn a customer's loyalty, you need to make that human connection so he or she will look forward to returning, again and again.

Unfortunately, the people working in that antique store didn't seem very interested in living up to the promise posted on their sign. They barely said hello. They were talking among themselves while we looked around. They didn't seem to notice or care when, after 15 minutes, we left—as strangers.

Some of the items in the store truly interested us. Perhaps if the staff had been friendlier and engaged us in conversation, we might have lingered longer and found something we liked enough to buy. But no one feels like browsing when the staff is ignoring you and chatting about who did what with whom last Friday night. We just didn't feel particularly welcome there. So we decided to visit the next antique store; there were several on the block, and we thought perhaps we would find one where the staff might actually be happy to see us.

Customers can be very satisfied with your goods or services, but in my experience, goods and services are not really what every customer wants. Customers want a human connection. They want to feel welcome, whether in person or online. They want you to show an interest in them. Ultimately, they want to feel valued as people. There are basic human needs and connections we commonly share with all the people in our lives. Without making these kinds of connections with your customers, your business risks ending up like the North Carolina antique shop—a place filled with attractive and unique merchandise but one that fails to cultivate customer loyalty or any level of satisfaction.

My dad owned a men's clothing store for many years, and up until the day he retired, he always welcomed customers into his store the way he welcomed guests into our home. Whether he knew the customer or not, he offered each one the same wide, inviting smile. For regulars at Murray's Men's Shop, the smile was followed by handshakes and big hugs. My dad liked to ask his customers about themselves and how they were, because hearing about someone's new job or recent vacation was so much more important to him than the color of the shirt or tie they wanted. He'd often share the latest joke he'd just heard, and my memories of working there as a teenager are filled as much with friendly banter and laughter as they are stocking and selling clothes.

Today when I lead one of my customer service workshops, I always begin with a simple exercise inspired by my dad's example. Imagine you are hosting a block party. You meet some new neighbors who have just moved in and invite them into your home. What would you say or do to make these guests feel welcome? Workshop participants have offered dozens of different responses to this question over the years, but most commonly suggest offering to take a guest's coat, fixing a drink, or giving a tour of their house. The point of the exercise is to remind participants that every one of us already possesses a natural instinct for making guests feel comfortable and welcome. The challenge is to extend that natural instinct from the home to the workplace.

Regrettably, most people aren't very good at treating customers as though they were guests in their home. Good customer service remains a rarity as a result. Even in places where one might reasonably expect to be treated well, I am continually surprised at the inability of customer service representatives to treat people courteously, as their welcomed and honored guests.

A few examples:

- The grumpy woman behind the will-call window at one of New York's most prestigious museums, snapping at customers as though they were criminals trying to sneak into Fort Knox.

- The sales associate at an exclusive bridal shop who "greeted" our friend's daughter and her group of excited relatives and brides-maids with an abrupt and unsmiling "Which one is the bride?"

- The harried clerk in the children's department at a famous department store who responded this way to the news that we were buying a gift for a newborn infant: "I'm busy right now. Why don't you look through the merchandise yourselves?"

I understand that retail workers are often stressed and busy. But how difficult is it to smile, say hello, and introduce yourself before identifying and congratulating the lucky bride? Why not offer a gracious word or two about how wonderful it is to be shopping for a newborn baby before excusing yourself with a hurried promise to be right back? And why would you treat museumgoers—possibly among the most patient and well-mannered group of customers you will ever find—with such disrespect?

Somehow, these workers have lost touch with their significance in the lives of the people they serve. A bridal shop is a place where lifelong dreams become reality. The shoppers in a children's section have one thing on their minds—a tiny new life that means the world to them. And how upsetting is it to be treated in an uncultured fashion while visiting a virtual temple of culture? In each case, these associates are unwelcoming because their supervisors have not trained them about the importance of making a human connection in the workplace—the human connection they likely have little trouble making when they invite guests into their homes.

First-time customers in particular need specialized attention, which my dad always understood very well. He would explain in detail the type of merchandise that he carried, recommended where to park during their next visit, and share when the next seasonal sale would begin. He even told them about his upcoming buying trips. My dad approached every stranger as a possible lifetime customer and future friend. He was authentically dedicated to helping people and creating relationships. Running a men's haberdashery was merely the medium through which he achieved this purpose.

Although it's not realistic to expect every sales associate to aspire to this level of relatedness to customers, there is much to be learned from my dad's example and those of many fine customer service professionals like him. Each loyal customer you have today was at some point a first-time visitor. If you fail to treat every new customer as well as you would your most loyal customer, you will never know how many potential lifetime customers you have turned away.

It all begins with hope

It may sound obvious, but if you wish to make a human connection with a customer—in person, on the phone, or online—then the most important thing to remember is each individual's *humanity*. Human beings come to you with hope in their hearts. They need or want something they haven't found elsewhere, and they hope you have the answer. Perhaps they are looking for the perfect Valentine's present, a watch for their son's graduation, or a gift for friends who just moved into a new home. Your job is to give them hope that they've come to a place where their problem or desire will be addressed in a helpful, friendly manner.

"Hope" can be defined as the expectation of a future positive or constructive event. We always hope for the best. When your kids are born, you have hope they will be healthy and live long and happy lives. Then they grow up and you hope their happiness will continue. Even in instances of serious illnesses, human beings rely on their fundamental need for hope as a way to maintain focus and keep their spirits up. That's why you must offer hope at the start of any relationship if you want that relationship to be sustained over time.

Offering hope begins with a welcoming smile. A smile is so important in business that a 2004 psychology study actually identified the value of a smile in dollars and cents. Participants were found to be willing to pay twice as much for a drink after being exposed briefly to photos of happy, smiling faces.[9] The pictures were mixed with images of grim and frowning faces, and they flashed by so fast that the participants were unaware of the effect the smiles were having. As Roger Dooley wrote in his Neuromarketing blog, "I think the study does show that even a tiny elevation of mood, so small that it is imperceptible to the subjects, could affect their spending. This means that the manager who trains her employees to smile is on the right track."[10]

I coach frontline associates to smile by asking them to imagine how they would greet their best friend after a long vacation. That's the kind of eager smile that can raise your customers' spirits and make them feel truly welcome. Smiling works in telephone greetings, as well, because callers can "feel" your enthusiasm over the phone. Smiles are so powerful that human beings can sense a smile just by the sound of your voice.

Welcoming sales associates will smile first and then introduce themselves by name. Even if associates wear name tags, an introduction is always important. In a contact center environment, it's helpful to train phone agents to introduce themselves twice—once at the beginning of the call and then again later in the conversation. Contact center customers frequently don't hear the agent's name at first or they quickly forget the name because they're preoccupied with their reason for calling. So it's a good idea, after hearing the reason for the call, for the phone agent to say, "Once again, my name is Mary, and I will be happy to help you with that."

One of my favorite recommendations for giving customers hope is for the frontline associate to include the key phrase "I can help you with that." Help is a broad concept. It might be that the associate needs to check with another employee or supervisor, get back to the customer later with additional information, or even refer the customer to a competitor who might have exactly what he or she is looking for. The online shoe retailer Zappos is one of a handful of companies that trains the contact center staff to make referrals to competitors as a way of being helpful to customers. It's as though they've taken a page from *Miracle on 34th Street*, when Kris Kringle at Macy's sent a customer to the competing Gimbels for a better pair of skates.

Maintaining an overall welcoming environment can be a challenge in a busy brick-and-mortar store. When there's a sudden rush of customers, it can be easy to ignore one customer while offering welcoming attention to another. Juggling multiple customers, however, is a simple and teachable skill. When someone enters your store while you are waiting on another customer, that person can see you're busy. What he or she needs in that moment is acknowledgment. It takes just a couple of seconds to say, "Hi! I will be with you shortly," and it makes a world of difference.

Once associates offer a smile and a greeting, they should next always see the customer as a person first and a customer second. Personalizing the experience with the customer is an effective way to build rapport. Perhaps someone is wearing a bright scarf, a beautiful coat, or a sports jersey. By observing and commenting on something that is specific or unique to that individual, associates can begin a dialogue.

The key is to phrase your comment in a way that is genuine. Say "I love your hat!" only if you really love it. Even if it's not your taste, you can still authentically admire it. Any question or observation that demonstrates an interest in the customer's personal experience ("Is it still raining outside?" "How old is your baby?" "Your little boy is so well behaved!") will show the customer that you want to make a human connection.

There's a common assumption that younger people aren't so interested in these kinds of conversations. But I'm confident that if a salesperson asks a teenager how he likes his new phone, the question will make him feel welcomed and acknowledged. If that same boy was wearing a cool T-shirt and the associate asked him where he got it, I'm sure that would be the beginning of a conversation and a potential sale.

I once walked into a restaurant with my friend Karen, and the hostess immediately asked Karen about her coat. Karen's story about how her mother had bought the coat in Paris marked the start of a delightful conversation that established a bond among all of us—and a bond with the restaurant, as well. I became a regular customer partly because of Lynn, the hostess, and the conversation we had about Karen's coat. From such simple exchanges relationships can be created and repeat business generated.

Training for welcoming

Not everyone is as naturally welcoming and observant as Lynn. But it's easy to educate most associates and improve their welcoming skills. Simple role-playing exercises can be the best way to train your staff in the talent of observation and conversation. Have your associates hold a meeting before your operation opens to the public. Ask them to notice what everyone in the group is wearing: a new pair of glasses, a colorful scarf, a different kind of headset, or a belt with an interesting buckle.

Another exercise encourages your associates to see things from the customer's point of view. Pair up your associates and have partners share about a recent shopping experience. Then ask them to describe the underlying emotion in that experience. Did they feel welcome? Did they leave happy? Or, did they feel dismissed, ignored, or rejected? During your daily staff huddles, ask associates to discuss their experiences about their favorite stores and e-commerce sites. Encourage them to recall what they liked. The members of your team will likely recognize how their positive experiences all started with a friendly smile, an easy-to-navigate website, or some other welcoming trigger that created a good first impression.

The concept of welcoming is just as critical in a call center environment. Customers contact the company because they have problems they wish they didn't have or questions that need to be answered. They are wary about who's going to pick up or whether an automated system is going to start taking them through a dozen menu options. When a person calls, that interaction is an opportunity to get the customer excited to do business with that company. Too many organizations don't make that initial contact hassle free.

The goal is not to create a relationship with every interaction. The goal is to invite a relationship. Some people are natural welcomers, like my dad. They enjoy engaging with people, and that's one of the reasons they choose to work in customer service. Many other sales associates behave in a somewhat robotic way. They go through the motions of what's asked of them, without any emotion. These are the people who benefit most from the kind of training exercises previously described. They are good, well-meaning employees who have never been effectively educated on how important it is to make an emotional connection with the customer.

On the other hand, psychologists say that some people are not naturally "emotionally expressive." Asking such people to act friendly if they don't feel friendly has been shown to lead to job burnout and even depression.[11] That's why it's so important to hire the right people for customer-facing positions. Once the significance of welcoming is recognized, then it is critical to explore how your hiring and recruiting practices can be changed to attract more innate welcomers. Perhaps hiring practices should be reoriented so that experience and competence with point-of-sale technology (which can be taught) are less important than a welcoming attitude (which is not as teachable). Identify the natural welcomers on your team and ask them to invite their friends to apply for jobs. Welcomers tend to have friends who are naturally outgoing and engaging.

Back in my father's day, it took a long time to accumulate customer goodwill. Today, through social media, first-time customer feedback is instantaneous and shared for all the world to see. No matter the medium of customer interaction—call center, website, or brick-and-mortar retail—a crucial initial step for any business is to ensure that the right people are hired who can make the best first impression.

Welcoming technology

When call centers first gained popularity in the 1980s, the idea behind the new technology was to make the customer experience more pleasant and efficient. Automated systems in their initial stages were designed to route calls to the first available agent as quickly as possible. Following a set of touch-tone prompts was considered a great way to ensure that the customer would find the person best suited to offer help.

Unfortunately, automated response systems are now more commonly used to minimize customer expectations for personalized help. These systems put customers on hold to hear advertising messages or, at their worst, tell customers to call back another time. I think that's a terrible practice. If hold times are longer than a couple of minutes, your organization is communicating a message to customers that their time and business are not valuable. Thanks to super-telephonic technology and flexible employment of remote or home-based agents, there is no reason why call centers can't be properly staffed.

I was surprised to get one such off-putting "Please call back later" message from a company that is usually very good with customer service: American Express. I really wanted to talk with someone, so I ignored the instruction and asked to be connected to a live representative and, voila, a person answered almost immediately. I was left with the distinct impression that American Express was using that "call back later" recording just to discourage phone calls and to prompt customers to use the website instead.

Sometimes call volumes are unmanageable, and in those cases I recommend that companies offer customers the option of leaving a telephone number so that a representative can call back later. Then the callers who are not in a hurry to speak to someone right away will have an option other than endlessly waiting on hold.

The same welcoming principles apply to that most basic of phone technologies—the outgoing message itself. The script for any outgoing message can offer the telephonic equivalent of a smile and an introduction. Each caller should be greeted with a friendly voice and positive, welcoming words. Word choice matters. There is no need to speak in the negative, such as "Sorry, we are closed," when the same information can be expressed more positively as "We are so glad you called us today and would be happy to help you tomorrow when we are open. Please leave your name and number and the best time to reach you."

The voice selected to deliver the message is as important as the message itself. Have one of your friendliest-sounding associates make the recording or, better yet, do it professionally so you can find that special tone that both is welcoming and reflects your company's brand.

Welcoming might be more important with e-commerce than elsewhere. Why? E-commerce makes it very easy for a frustrated customer to flee. When I visit an online site, in a matter of seconds I can be annoyed, and your competitor is a mere click away. On the other hand, when I physically enter a store, I might be willing to put up with some indifference from the sales staff, just to complete my purchase. Web designers should understand that e-commerce shoppers experience strong emotions when searching a website or navigating an app. E-commerce makes the shopping experience faster and more efficient than ever before, but speed and efficiency are not more important than making a human connection that will keep shoppers from a competitor just a key stroke away.

There are so many ways to welcome a customer with the first click of the mouse: make it easy for a customer to get help; to find the "Contact us" button, telephone number, or hours of operation; or to open a pop-up chat screen to get questions answered instantly. There's a lot to be said for keeping things simple. Software maker Basecamp.com, for instance, decided to take a cue from what works, says designer Jason Fried. "I've always found it interesting that some of the most popular sites on the Web—Amazon, eBay, Craigslist, Wikipedia, to name a few—are often very heavy on the text and very light on the imagery. These sites won't win any design awards, but they seem to communicate very clearly to their intended audience. They don't try too hard; they just are what they are. There's no shame in that."[12] A lot of web design is too fancy for its own good. Slick and overdesigned features frequently make those sites slow to load and difficult to figure out—in a word, unwelcoming.

Online welcoming extends to e-mail, too. A friendly confirmation e-mail expressing appreciation for the customer's business is a great first step. Review every e-mail script. Registering for the site, resending passwords, confirming orders, and providing delivery information are all opportunities to communicate welcoming messages. Sign each e-mail with an associate's name to make the message more personal, and never send out an e-mail that tells the recipient "DO NOT REPLY." This is a point that bears repeating later in chapter 5. Where else in your life would you ever give someone a message that instructs the recipient not to reply? That's no way to begin a relationship of any kind.

Welcoming environment

I have friends who will never sit down to order at a restaurant until they first inspect the bathroom. If it's spotless and fully stocked with supplies, they then feel that the kitchen is probably clean and well run, too. It's only natural to assume the opposite, however, if the bathroom is filthy, with broken faucets and paper towels strewn on the floor. First impressions should welcome customers by appealing to all senses: a place should look, feel, and smell clean, with pleasant music playing and the thermostat set at a comfortable temperature.

With that kind of welcoming environment, customers will want to do business with you. I once overheard a woman tell her friend she had just gotten off the phone with the receptionist at a medical office where she was making her first appointment. She told her friend she was glad the receptionist was so nice and friendly because, in her experience, that meant that her new doctor would also be caring and empathic. Having a receptionist who can radiate that sense of concern—even over the phone— announces to the world that caring is something highly valued by you and your employees. It's the kind of signal that people are naturally attuned to pick up.

Years ago TD Bank (formerly Commerce Bank) made its branches more welcoming by eliminating those rope-and-stanchion corrals that herd customers toward the next available teller. As banks go, TD branches feel warm and homey. There are lollipops on the counter and coin-changing machines specially designed even for children. The interiors in some branches pay tribute to the local neighborhood. On 14th Street and Fifth Avenue in Manhattan, there is a large mural of the very same street from the late 1800s with horse-drawn carriages and women wearing big hats and carrying parasols. Every time I go into the bank, I admire and appreciate the historical perspective.

Another feature at TD Bank is that tellers are not stationed behind bulletproof windows, as they are at competing bank branches in the neighborhood. The idea is to offer customers a more welcoming retail-like experience. After a spree of bank robberies in 2009, New York's police commissioner criticized the bank for not installing glass barriers between customers and tellers. But the company "stuck to its guns," so to speak.[13] After all, everything about the welcoming first impression should encourage customers to feel comfortable because that's the initial step toward building an ongoing relationship. TD Bank determined that treating your customers like cattle does not provide an atmosphere in which connections can be created.

In order to be truly welcoming, you must fully understand what's important to your customers. Wal-Mart, for instance, once tried to tidy up its stores by taking stacks of boxes out of the aisles and giving the shelves a cleaner and less cluttered look. But sales fell and Wal-Mart officials learned the hard way that their discount shoppers feel more comfortable with overcrowded aisles and overstuffed shelves. The "cleaner" look at Wal-Mart stores had an intimidating effect and discouraged bargain hunters from buying.

On the other hand, most department store shoppers have higher expectations for tidiness and order. Brian Sozzi, chief executive at Belus Capital Advisors, has become a popular blogger by taking pictures of Kmart and Sears store interiors and their disarray—typified by empty shelves, shoddy displays, and an overall feel of dirt and disorder.[14] From his perspective, Kmart and Sears stores have become so poorly managed and unappealing that investing in their parent company stock is unwise.

How you choose to express your store policies plays a role in determining whether your customers feel like welcome guests. Stores with fragile items, such as antique shops, should never post those "If you break it, you've bought it" signs. You can encourage your clumsy customers to avoid handling the merchandise by making sure prices are readily visible and displaying a message such as "Please ask a sales associate to help with handling fragile items." All the signage in your store should similarly emphasize the positive. It's much more welcoming to read "We will be happy to exchange or refund your item within 7 days" rather than "NO RETURNS AFTER 7 DAYS."

Employees should keep an eye out for customers with special needs or problems. If a person is carrying a few shopping bags, ask whether he or she needs help so as not to be encumbered. Keeping small bottles of cold water on hand for the customer who just walked in on a hot day will relay a message of welcome and let the person know you would like him or her to stay. Employees should be instructed to open the store a few minutes early if they see a customer waiting outside in the rain. That's one way to make an instant friend. It tells customers that they are more important than the opening time posted on the door.

Even during those times when you can't offer customers what they're looking for, you can offer all your customers the assurance that yours is a place where they will always feel welcome. If you can hold on to that thought and share it often with your colleagues and staff, you will have taken that first important step toward generating repeat business. There is a distinction between customer satisfaction and customer retention. One customer may have a satisfactory "no complaints" shopping experience and then promptly forget all about you and your store. Another customer might leave empty-handed because you don't stock the item he or she wanted, but this "dissatisfied" customer will never forget the welcoming smile and helpful attitude with which he or she was greeted.

In that sense, true customer loyalty, the goal of every successful business, should never be confused with customer satisfaction. "Loyal customers are very different from satisfied customers," writes Joanna Ellis of Ellis Partners real estate consultancy. "Consider whom you are loyal to. Surely you'll answer family and friends. Why? Because of the emotional bond you have with them. Your family and friends can do things you may not like, but you stay loyal because of that connection. The same applies with customer loyalty."[15]

This simple equation holds true for every type of business, from a B2B sole proprietorship to a global e-commerce company. If you don't treat your customers with the same welcoming respect and regard with which you treat friends and family, you will never have a chance to earn their true loyalty.

Take a good look at any company that is known for being "loved" by legions of loyal customers. You will discover that the company has instituted any number of consistent procedures and practices that assure customers of their importance—little things that most companies neglect to include in their overall customer experience strategies. It's time to take a look at this aspect of your offerings to your customers. If your follow-up communications are careless and somehow suggest that you take your customers for granted, those customers will never love your company and will never give you their loyalty.

Power Points Worth Repeating

- To earn a customer's loyalty, make a human connection.

- Always welcome customers the way you would welcome guests in your home.

- First-time customers in particular need special attention.

- Give customers the hope that they have come to the right place to find what they want or have a problem solved.

- Saying "I can help you with that" helps fulfill that hope.

- Personalizing the experience builds rapport.

- The goal is to invite a relationship, not necessarily create one.

- Ensure that your associates are capable of making the best first impression.

- Long hold times communicate that the customer's time and business are not valuable.

- The very nature of e-commerce makes it easy for customers to flee.

- Sending "Do Not Reply" e-mails turns off customers instead of welcoming them.

- True customer loyalty should never be confused with customer satisfaction.

2

Give Me Your Full Attention

My wife and I were meeting friends for brunch at the Brownstone Pancake Factory in Edgewater, New Jersey, so we asked to be seated at a booth for four. Then our friends didn't show up (a missed communication), and we felt bad and a little embarrassed that there were just two of us in this big booth while larger parties were waiting in a rather long line to be seated.

Ashley, our waitress, gave what I'll always remember as the perfect response. "No worries," she said. "Instead of four, there will be 'three' of us for breakfast." It was a clever and delightful way of telling us that we were welcome to stay at the booth. More importantly, Ashley demonstrated that she recognized our embarrassment and made our feelings the sole focus of her attention. She didn't treat us as a problem that needed to be solved—two people at a booth for four with many customers waiting in line. She put our concerns before her own and paid attention to what was important in that moment. A seemingly little thing but certainly memorable.

Listening is fundamental

Customers crave attention. They want and need to feel that you're interested in them. The best kind of selling is selling that reveals the customer's needs and wants through meaningful dialogue. By offering your full, undivided attention, you invite the customer to participate in that conversation.

Fundamentally, giving your full attention requires an ability to acutely listen. You've already made the customer feel welcome. Now you want the customer to feel that your primary interest is his or her needs—not your own to make a sale. By listening patiently, you offer the customer that important feeling that he or she comes first.

When I started my company in the late 1980s, our first client was Ricoh Corporation, where my contact was a vice president named Wayne. Whenever I visited Wayne to discuss a new service or review results from a recent survey, our meetings never started on time. But once I stepped into his office and sat down, he always listened intently to what I had to say. There was never a rush to our conversation or a nervous glance at a watch. Wayne respected me and my expertise, and he was eager to hear what I had to say.

I realized after several meetings that Wayne was always late because he treated every visitor to his office exactly the same. Everyone he met received his full attention, and it was worth waiting for.

Joe Girard, the *Guinness Book*'s world record–holder for retail sales, had a lot in common with my old friend Wayne when it came to the art of undivided attention. Between 1963 and 1978, Girard sold a record-breaking 13,001 vehicles for a Detroit-area Chevrolet dealership. His all-time high was 18 sales in a single day, when most car salespeople sold seven or eight per month. There was such a long line of people outside Joe's office that eventually he required customers to make an appointment in advance just to see him. Just like Wayne's, Joe's attention was worth the wait. He noted in an interview, "People may have had to wait for an appointment, but when I was with them, I was with them body and soul."[16]

One of the most useful business courses I ever took was about the practice of active listening. At the start of any conversation, active listening helps build a human connection by detecting and then acknowledging the other person's underlying emotions. "By listening, you get into their shoes," says Linda Adams of Gordon Training International. "[You] understand their frame of reference, different though it may be from your own."[17]

Every individual who visits your store, contacts your call center, clicks on your website, or sends you an e-mail is in a specific emotional state at that moment. In order to build a human connection and bond, listen carefully and respond to that emotion *before* addressing the actual reason the customer has come to you.

For example, if someone is calling customer support because a new gadget isn't working properly, that customer is likely to be annoyed, frustrated, or, in some cases, very upset. The representative might say, "Mrs. Smith, I understand you are frustrated. Let's see how I can help resolve this problem." Once you've assured Mrs. Smith that you understand how she is feeling, a foundation has been laid for further conversation. Even if her problem is one that can't be immediately remedied, she is much more likely to be grateful for your attempt to help, simply because you've acknowledged how she feels.

Even if the representative misses the mark and identifies the wrong emotion, active listening will get you points for trying. Mrs. Smith will be quick to say, "No, I'm not angry. I'm just really annoyed." Your interest in her emotional state gives room to respond, "Well, I'm very sorry you're annoyed and probably disappointed. Let's see what I can do to help you." Active and present interest in her emotional well-being allows the conversation to continue.

The important thing to remember is this: it's not enough to offer your full attention—the customer must *feel* it. That is the definition of active listening and what it can achieve. When a customer's underlying emotion is identified right off the bat, it is reassuring that he or she is seen as a person first and a customer second. A crucial step has been taken toward establishing trust through a meaningful dialogue. I can't emphasize enough how valuable this point is, even in terms of efficiency. Research by the Customer Contact Council has found that 24 percent of repeat calls from customers take place solely because on the prior call, customers were unable to make an emotional connection with the phone agent.[18]

While researching my first book, I made "mystery shopper" visits to hundreds of retail establishments across the country and initiated dozens of consumer support calls and e-mails to companies in a variety of industries. In order to assess the "listening quality" I perceived in all these exchanges, I relied on the following five key phrases:

"This is my first time in your store."

"I just moved into the neighborhood."

"My friend suggested I might like your merchandise."

"I have never used your website before."

"This is the first time I'm calling your contact center."

If you want to test your employees' listening skills, these are the phrases that should always elicit a response appealing to the customer's emotional state of mind. A representative who ignores the cue and doesn't say, "Welcome to the neighborhood! "What brings you here today?" or " I understand this is the first time you are calling us; what can I do to help you?" has failed to show interest in the customer as a person and will likely also fail to develop any bonds that create loyal customers.

Paying attention of course extends beyond a phone call. A crowded store is a good example. What to do with busy customers who don't like to wait? Take a page from Wayne and Joe and don't divide your attention. Avoid the temptation to multitask. It's not really possible to give your "full" attention to two people at once, anyway. It's better to acknowledge, ask them to wait, and then make sure that someone else is around to offer a seat or perhaps something to drink. Regulars will not mind waiting if past experience tells them they will enjoy the benefits of your full attention when it's their turn.

Waiting is a problem. People often feel uneasy while waiting because psychologically they are not in control. One way to restore a feeling of control is to offer choices. For instance, if a customer calls your company or store and there is an automated voice system, now certainly the norm, customers appreciate if they are provided with an estimated hold time and an option to have a return call. The callback should be at a convenient hour for the customer. Having a choice is a deep human need that can't be ignored. Choice preserves a person's sense of autonomy and comfort. One study found that blood donors perceived significantly less discomfort from a needle stick when they were allowed to select the arm from which the blood would be drawn. Having that seemingly meaningless choice reduced their actual perception of pain.[19]

Another area of concern is our smartphone and how most of us are now joined at the hip to that device. How many times have you walked into a store and found you were ignored while a sales associate was busy composing a text message? We are all guilty of this behavior. I often divide my attention while multitasking, by texting and talking at the same time. I also know I would be a better listener if I were to silence my phone every time I wanted or needed to listen to a friend, coworker, or family member. In fact, making a habit of each of these practices— active listening, acknowledging prior obligations, offering choices—has the potential to improve your rapport with all the people in your life. Try using them with everyone you know, and notice the difference in the quality of your relationships.

When Nathan Lustig, cofounder of Entrustet, did just that, he recalled, "As I got in the habit of really listening to people, I noticed things began to change. People remember me more often. They tell me I'm a good listener. They ask for my advice. They offer to make connections for me. My friends think I'm more interesting, even if I'm not talking. I notice things and see better opportunities for myself, my business, and for other people."[20]

Offering your full attention is so valuable that it's more than a mere sales strategy. It's a vital life skill that is getting more important by the day. Commentators have noted how, with so much instant information available around the clock, we have moved past the Information Age into the Attention Age. Information has become so abundant that it has made attention scarce. Paying attention has become the differentiator.

Jason Fried, author of the best-selling book *ReWork* and designer of Basecamp.com, whom we met in chapter 1, recalls how Disney executives hired him to study which of the features at the company's theme parks most reliably captured the attention of small children and toddlers. What he discovered was that all the bigger-than-life walking cartoon characters and animatronic creature displays were no match for

Mom and Dad's cell phones. When the parents took out their phones, that's all the children were interested in, no matter what was going on around them. What the children really needed was their parents' full attention, and not even the features of the world's greatest theme parks could distract them from that basic need.

Providing full attention in all channels

Our firm conducted research for a client who wanted to compare his company's service and support for e-mail inquiries with that of 20 other companies, each of which was a customer service leader in its respective industry. For this project, we developed 10 different e-mail scenarios to send to the target companies and then measured the speed and quality of their responses. One test e-mail began, "I just had a baby and I have a question about your product." Another e-mail asked, "My dog accidentally chewed and digested part of your packaging. Do I need to worry?"

When the e-mail responses were tabulated from all 20 of these leading companies, we were surprised how poorly the e-mails responded to the human, emotional content of the inquiries. Of the 20 companies that were sent the message that began "I just had a baby," only one e-mail response contained the line "Congratulations on your new arrival!" All the others merely responded to the specific request for information. They paid no attention at all to the new mother's most obvious underlying emotion, joy about her newborn.

To their credit, most of the companies replied almost instantly that the dog that had eaten the company's packaging should be seen by a veterinarian right away. However, two of the companies waited more than two weeks to deliver that message, obviously long after such advice would have been of any help at all. In fact, such a slow response to an emergency of that kind might actually be worse than if the company had not responded at all.

There's really no excuse for not giving full, personal attention in an e-mail response. The customer's message is right there in front of you. There is never a need to ask customers to repeat what they just said. With online chat, Twitter, Facebook, and Pinterest, the written word offers vast opportunities to show your customers that you are listening and listening carefully. There are many technologies that provide sentiment analysis of text to help representatives quickly discern the proper emotions and respond appropriately. For social media, the automation of this process also helps representatives respond quickly to fraudulent inquiries.

One important purpose of this book is to remind readers how important it is to embrace the human connection in everything we do. In order to truly gain people's attention and trust, it is essential that you communicate your attention and trust through the channels and media your customers prefer. With so many gadgets, apps, and innovative services being released every day, a critical component of customer loyalty is creating that emotional bond, and listening helps accomplish that goal.

Social media can be a challenging channel in this respect. A Pew study says that 28 percent of women will comment on brands through social media, while another study says that 65 percent of women use social media to research their purchases. As mobile phones get smarter and more powerful, these numbers are destined to climb with each year. Consider that women are responsible for the purchase of 80 percent of household goods and the opportunities for gaining competitive advantage through social media are enormous.

The good news is that most companies have tremendous room for improvement in this area. I say good news because it is very likely that your company has not even begun to maximize existing opportunities to attract and retain customers until everyone at every level of the company is giving his or her full attention in all available channels. I discussed how I researched my first book with hundreds of mystery shopper exchanges. In almost 90 percent of the cases, my encounters could have been enhanced. Yes, in my opinion, 90 percent of all customer-company interactions, whether face-to-face or on the phone or Internet, could have been more effective in building a human connection.

There are some excellent models for using mobile texts and social media in order to be attentive to customers. Qdoba Mexican Grill discovered that by delivering coupons to smartphones at certain times of the day or week, sales and demand increased. Late-night text campaigns near universities saw a nearly 40 percent redemption rate on these coupons simply because they caught the students' attention when their stomachs were growling. The normal rates of coupon redemption averaged just 16 percent.

On Twitter, the staff at @AskCapitalOne greets its followers with a different message every morning at 6 a.m., inviting them to tweet their help requests. One typical welcoming message read: "Good Morning! We're back in the office, coffee in hand, and ready to help. Tweet us if you need us!" Although these messages may be automated, the responses are not. So one day when @zombiehippy tweeted "where do I check my miles reward[?]" he received a response within 20 minutes from the @AskCapitolOne team: "Hey there! Once you're logged in, click on Rewards Summary!" The quick response to @zombiehippy serves as assurance to all Capital One customers that the company's Twitter team is ready to offer its prompt attention if needed.

We are living through a time of transition when it comes to technology. Sixty percent of people think that technology "makes us feel more connected," according to a Yankelovich Monitor survey, but 40 percent think exactly the opposite, that "technology has made us more isolated from each other." So the odds are that 60 percent of customers expect to connect with you online and through social media because they feel positively toward the technology. Customers expect your company to be responsive to the channels they prefer in their daily lives and will not trust you if they don't feel they are being heard. With more than half of the population using online technologies to communicate, too much is at stake not to do it right.

I listened to a demonstration of a new call center system incorporating artificial intelligence with a human analyst. In the sample recording, a customer was reconfirming his stay at a hotel property where he had never been before, and the automated system conversed with him very naturally. The promise of such software is that it can provide a higher degree of accuracy than human phone agents and therefore a better customer experience.

I can understand that customers might not necessarily want to talk to a machine, but if an interaction is smooth and thorough, I can also see how such a system can leave a positive impression. For some industries more than others, there is great promise in this kind of AI-enabled customer service. If an automated system offers me a set of messages tailored to my specific customer information (and doesn't force me to repeat myself), then I'm happy to have my call handled in an efficient manner, even if I never speak to a human being.

My only quibble with the hotel booking call was that the automated system ignored how this was the customer's first visit to the property. With the help of some simple predictive data (a growing trend in artificial intelligence), the automated voice could have added, "I know this is the first time you are staying at our hotel, and I hope you enjoy this location."

Such a sentiment would have been personal and made the traveler feel more welcome and appreciated.

Speech recognition technology is destined to become increasingly more sophisticated and capable of understanding a wider variety of language dialects in noisy environments where today such systems don't work. Gartner Consulting has predicted that among the top technology trends on the horizon, "the smart machine era will be the most disruptive in the history of [information technology]."[21]

Everyone's concern, then, should be focused on how to incorporate this new technology to enhance the human connection. New technology should always be tested and retested through customer feedback. Fine-tune the experience using predictive responses to ensure a smoother and more customized interaction so that when AI can't provide the answer, it locates a live agent to assist. Ultimately, call centers depend on well-trained call agents to listen to customers' emotions and respond with a true human touch.

Remember what's at stake

My wife and I were shopping for a folding table. Why? We had invited 16 people to a holiday dinner, and our dining room table seats only 12. So we were short a table. In a sense, we weren't looking for a piece of furniture. Our mission was to create enough room for family and friends to celebrate together.

Every purchase has a human story behind it. If employees are trained to recognize that there can be deep and highly personal motivations behind even the most mundane customer contact—each visit, phone call, e-mail, and tweet—it will be easier to remember the importance of making a human connection with those customers. "If you're in the brick-and-mortar business," says shopping center developer Rick Caruso, "you need to be in the hospitality business. Consider the human needs you meet every day."[22] A McKinsey report says that 70 percent of buying experiences are based on how the customer *feels* he or she is being treated.[23] I'm surprised this number isn't closer to 90 percent.

Creating relationships takes trust, one of the most critical ingredients for building customer loyalty. When trust is broken, customer allegiance is lost and rarely can be revived. Building trust begins with active listening. It continues with subsequent steps furthering the relationship. I've compiled a list of what I call the five pillars of trust. Some of the points are covered in depth later in the book but are so important they bear mentioning more than once.

- **Active listening**—Hearing another person's words, detecting the underlying emotion, and then responding with acknowledgement provide a strong foundation for building any long-lasting relationship.

- **Share personal feelings**—Let customers know your personal opinion if they request it. If an outfit doesn't look good, a dish isn't the best on the menu, or you know that the quality of an electronic gadget is suspect, share those thoughts. These are stepping-stones for continual trust.

- **Recommend competitors**—Make sure your representatives know about similar products found elsewhere that might be a better fit for your customers. This ties in with the two tips above. Your associate is listening and sharing, keeping the customer's best interests at the forefront.

- **Stand behind your products**—Guarantee satisfaction. Make sure that policies are in place so that your representatives can rise to the occasion when a product fails to please. Quantify the extent to which your organization is truly quality driven and customer focused.

- **Follow through**—Keeping customers informed throughout the ordering and delivery process should be part of the value you offer. Over the long run, following through, following up, and keeping customers in the loop are the links in the chain of trust that can never be broken.

It's easy to forget the benefits of relationship building through listening. For example, finding out how a new customer found your place of business or the number for your company or your e-commerce site is some of most important market research you can ever conduct. Did the person read a review on a social media site, walk by, or find you on Google? Knowing the answers to these questions can help you make all sorts of important decisions. And the research is free; just ask.

First-time customers don't expect to find relationships when they walk into a store, call a customer service department, or make an e-commerce purchase. They have no expectation that the encounter will be personalized or memorable, which is exactly why, when it happens, customers remember and return. In our social media era, the experience is reported for all their Facebook friends, Twitter followers, and Yelp readers to see. What if the opposite is true and you don't offer your customers the attention they deserve? Someone else will, and you'll never see or hear from them again.

My wife and I were shopping on the Pearl Street Mall in Boulder, Colorado, and went into a gallery whose window display caught our eye. The two store associates were paying intense attention—to their computers, not to us. They barely said hello, and we were the only people in the shop. It would have been so easy. We had some questions about a piece of pottery, and when we asked and tried to engage them, it definitely felt as if we were intruding—so disrespectful on their part. Did they think we weren't worth their time? Did they size us up and assume we weren't serious buyers?

We liked a particular bowl and wanted to know whether they shipped or could wrap it well so we could carry it with us on the plane. We actually felt uncomfortable interrupting and also weren't sure whether they would be indifferent to making sure our purchase was safe. So instead, my wife looked at the underside of the bowl, where a label had all the information we needed. We left the gallery and returned to our hotel, where we ordered it online. Our preference would have been to buy the piece in Boulder as a memento of our trip. But we couldn't wait to escape that art gallery where the owners had failed to train their staff properly. They did not pay attention to us at all. How often does this happen? Every day in most businesses. How much revenue is lost? I can only imagine.

Todd and Mike Shumaker of Confidential On-Site Paper Shredding in Illinois have compiled these 10 rules for giving full attention:[24]

1. **Posture begets performance**
   Always sit up straight and smile when you take a call; it shows.
   —Susan McGarvie, former Xerox employee

2. **Say it again**
   Acknowledge the customer's issue by relaying it back to him or her to make sure you understand what he or she is asking. It validates the customer and ensures that you understand the issue.
   —Tara Kachaturoff, *Personal Brand Essentials*

3. **Be you, not a script**
   Get off the script and LISTEN and respond to what's really going on.
   —Shel Horowitz, *Principled Profit*

4. Smile; they're listening

Smile while you are on the phone with a customer. It really does make a huge difference.

—Robyn Wright, Robynsonlineworld.com

5. Focus

Give them your full attention. Always treat clients you are speaking with as if they are your only clients.

—Phyllis Pometta, *Baby Swags*

6. Focus more

Focus on what they need, not what you "sell," and always give value added.

—Harriet Cohen, Training Solutions

7. Solutions aren't always necessary

Don't offer advice unless you're asked for it; often, customers, clients, and guests just want to talk and don't want your solution. It's refreshing to realize that you don't always have to fix everything.

—Robb Anderson, *La Villa Bonita Culinary Vacations*

8. Do you spell Bob with one or two o's?

Don't automatically call your customer by his or her first name; ask how he or she prefers to be addressed while you assist him or her.

—Ellen Schuster, MEd, CPCC, *The People Skills Expert*

9. No distractions

Turn OFF your cell phone. Don't even look at it or check to see who called when you are dealing with a customer.

—Andrea Baker, Voodoo Marketing

10. Give it to them two ways

Follow up with a phone call after communicating with a customer through e-mail.

—Melanie Haywood, CEO Listasaurus.com

Power Points Worth Repeating

- Customers crave attention; they need and want to feel you are interested in them.

- The best kind of selling reveals the customer's needs and wants through a meaningful dialogue.

- Listening patiently provides the customer with the feeling that he or she comes first.

- Every customer who contacts your company is in a specific emotional state.

- It's not enough to offer your full attention; the customer must feel it.

- People feel uneasy waiting because psychologically they are not in control.

- We have moved from the Information Age into the Attention Age.

- Communicate attention and trust through the channels your customers prefer.

- New technology should always be tested and retested through customer feedback.

- Every purchase has a story behind it.

- When trust is broken, customer allegiance is lost and rarely can be revived.

- Building trust begins with active listening.

- Finding out how a new customer found your business is critical market research.

Answer More Than My Question

One summer evening we were planning to meet some friends at a restaurant in rural upstate New York. We got lost on the way. The GPS was not helping, so when we found a fire station, we pulled in and asked for help. The man on duty was familiar with our destination and happy to give us detailed directions with all the important landmarks along the way.

Then the gentleman added some information that would end up making all the difference for us. He cautioned that we should ignore any construction detour signs. The road up ahead was indeed closed for repair but not for at least a mile beyond the point where the restaurant was located. If we obeyed the detour instructions, he said, we'd never get there.

We followed the man's directions and passed at least five signs that announced "Road Closed Ahead. Please Detour." If we had taken any of those detours, we would have been lost again and far past the restaurant. The trip could have turned out to be extremely frustrating, and we probably never would have met our friends. Instead, it was a relaxing drive, and we enjoyed the scenery along the way. We both felt such gratitude that the man at the fire station had been thoughtful enough to tell us about the detour signs. He more than answered our question.

When a customer asks questions, the sales associate is presented with an opportunity to build a relationship with someone who is fully engaged in the purchasing process. Questions are the customer's way of inviting you to become a valuable guide in his or her journey. A sales associate accepts that invitation by taking the time to anticipate the "detours" and other obstacles that might lie ahead. That's often the information that has the most profound effect on the customer.

The curiosity factor

"Yes" and "No." These one-word answers are worse than inadequate. They are so lacking in useful information that they can often mislead. In fact, they are such a reliable source of frustration that moviemakers have relied on them for decades as the linchpin for comic dialogue. This old joke has been used in more than one movie: A guest appears at the front desk of a charming country inn, where a small dog is reclining on the carpet. The guest asks, "Does your dog bite?" and the desk clerk replies absently, "No."

So the guest bends to pet the dog, which viciously snaps at his outstretched hand. "I thought you said your dog doesn't bite!" the alarmed guest exclaims.

The desk clerk replies, "Oh, that's not my dog."

How many times have you had a "that's not my dog" experience with a sales associate or a call center agent? "Why am I paying additional for this?" "Why didn't you tell me I didn't need this option?" "Why didn't you warn me the colors wouldn't match?" In each case, you're told, more or less: "You didn't ask." The responsibility is put back on you, the customer. Somehow you didn't phrase your question properly.

By anticipating the customer's need for additional information—information the customer didn't ask for—you become a source of direction and focus that will help that customer solve a tricky problem or fulfill the wish that brought him or her to you in the first place. Our research at TCFCR has shown that 95 percent of customers who are provided additional useful information are delighted with the interaction. That's because, first and foremost, you've demonstrated that you are listening, fulfilling that fundamental need of every customer. Then, if you can anticipate the customer's needs with your answer, you are able to create an experience that is unique and special.

In a contact center, you can train your agents to anticipate the needs of customers and provide that additional useful information. However, it can also be included in your knowledgebase software. For example, if someone is calling about a discontinued product, add some alternatives on that product's page for the representative to recommend. E-commerce sites offer numerous opportunities to provide customers with information. The website for Backcountry, the outdoor gear and clothing retailer, shows you not only what else is frequently purchased with the item you're viewing but also what other items have been purchased by customers who have viewed the same.

However, customers will not ask questions if you don't invite them to ask. You must make them feel comfortable asking, and not everyone does. For instance, I've found that many stores do not have their return policies prominently displayed. Perhaps these retailers fear that such signage would only encourage more returns. But the truth is that you need to know whether your customers are dissatisfied. In that sense, returns are an important aspect of customer feedback. A returned item can also become a moment of truth, when there's an opportunity to fortify your customer's loyalty or to lose it entirely.

Ariston Flowers in Manhattan includes the following note with all its floral arrangements: "We have built up an excellent reputation on beautiful flowers and prompt service. If we ever fail to meet your expectations, please let us know. It was a pleasure to give your order our personal attention."

Ariston creates beautiful arrangements, but on one occasion the florist really did fail to meet our expectations. A bouquet of roses was delivered to my wife, but the flowers started to wilt and lose petals after just two days. I called Ariston, and the woman on the line was apologetic in a friendly, upbeat manner. Within an hour, a new arrangement arrived at our door.

Without that note inviting me to let Ariston know of our disappointment with the roses, I doubt I would have bothered to call. But I also doubt I would have kept ordering flowers from Ariston in the future, because my last experience had not been good. That's why all businesses should make sure to tell customers that their satisfaction is guaranteed. Ariston will now continue to get all of my business and referrals to neighbors and friends—not because Ariston is perfect but because the company asked me to express my dissatisfaction, which ensured that even a bad experience had a positive outcome.

All along the customer journey, customers will tend to avoid asking questions unless they feel that associates are willing to offer their full attention. I enjoy talking to sales associates more than most people, but even I tend to fall back into nonengagement if I feel an associate is not up to the task. If there is an offer to help but in a bored or indifferent way, I'm more than likely to respond that I'm just looking.

That's why curiosity about the customer is one of the most important qualities to have at this stage of the customer journey. It is a stage that requires initiative and a little courage, but the best salespeople see it as an opportunity for interaction and creativity. It's a moment to consider options, test ideas, and fire the imagination. When you can partner with a customer to help that customer attain a goal, you have an opportunity to develop a truly emotional bond.

The best frontline employees have a natural curiosity to know more, if only because they enjoy helping people. The theme park industry understands this concept. Take a ride on one of those trams at Universal Studios and watch how the seasoned tour guides engage their passengers by asking them about themselves, what they've seen so far, and what excites them.

Tour guides recognize that every visitor arrives with his or her own individual outlook and expectations. You must get to know these things about your customers and appreciate them before you can ever anticipate customers' needs and give them fully informed, useful, and relevant answers to their questions.

You find great tour guides in every line of business. My dermatologist, Dr. Campbell, has a lot in common with those theme park guides. She's always asking me questions and not just about my health. She wants to know about movies I've seen or restaurant recommendations I might have, in order to know me better and to pass on what she learns to her other patients. The grandparents she sees are always happy to hear of some new, interesting place to take their grandchildren, and she finds out about such places from her other patients. Those patients come back to tell Dr. Campbell how much they appreciated that advice—which, strictly speaking, has *nothing* to do with her medical practice.

Or does it? The truth is that knowing all about her patients' lives makes her a better doctor. The more she knows about what's important to patients, the easier it is for her to treat them. She's also able to understand what might prevent them from complying with her instructions after they leave the office.

One of the most difficult tasks for any doctor is persuading patients to follow through on the prescribed treatment, whether it's taking medication regularly, remaining on a particular diet, or, in my dermatologist's case, applying topical medications with regularity and in exactly the right way. Because Dr. Campbell's patients feel that she listens to them, they listen to her. They do what the doctor recommends. They follow through with their treatments, and as a result, their conditions improve, and they conclude that she's an excellent doctor.

And Dr. Campbell *is* an excellent doctor. But results with her patients aren't entirely due to her soundness as a clinician. They are supported by her exceptional skills in customer service.

Forming the perfect answer

If a particular associate has just completed training and spent only a week on the job, that individual can still engage customers in meaningful dialogue. For such an employee, however, "I don't know" is an unhelpful response that breaks the dialogue, even if it reflects the truth. Instead, employees should be trained to say, "That's a good question. Let me find out for you." That way you express respect for the customer's question and communicate the sense that you are curious and want to get an answer on the customer's behalf. And, should the customer say, "Please, don't bother," the associate should follow through anyway and explain how it will help his or her training process.

Building a customer dialogue has a lot in common with the best practices in networking. One of my friends, Jack Killion, is a master executive coach who works with business leaders to improve their professional networking. Jack sees networking as a way to enrich one's life and requires only that you talk to everyone all the time and ask good questions when you are conversing. Jack always asks great questions, and if he had to coach retail associates, I'm sure his instructions would not differ from the coaching he offers top business leaders.

Here are Jack's tips for engaging anyone in conversation:

- Find something nice to say.

- Maintain eye contact.

- Ask a relevant question.

- Get them talking.

- Add humor. Don't always be deadly serious.

- Be positive, genuine, and likeable.

Jack has met so many interesting people in his life because he has a natural inquisitiveness. In customer service, there is a lot to gain from curiosity, because it is the only way to ensure that the customer is *totally* satisfied—a true predictor of loyalty. Xerox discovered that its "totally satisfied" customers were *six times* more likely to return than its "satisfied" customers.[25] Another study found that "totally satisfied" bank customers were 42 percent more likely to become loyal repeat customers over those who were merely satisfied.[26]

My father didn't need to see these studies to know that total satisfaction is the only satisfaction worth discussing. So much of what I learned about customer service came from my father exercising his curiosity about his customers and then seeing how he put that knowledge of the customer to work.

Drawing on what he learned or could quickly deduce about his customer, he would often locate the perfect product and then suggest additional items the customer hadn't even thought of. This practice was a world away from the common suggestive selling of robotically asking "And would you like fries with that?" or pushing extended warranties on customers. My father's suggestions were in direct response to what he'd learned about the customer, and even when customers weren't interested in buying, they enjoyed the interaction. They were gratified by my father's interest in them, and to that extent, they left his shop *totally* satisfied.

The authors of a *Harvard Business Review* article suggest that computer software can now replicate at scale the same thing my father used to do on an individual basis. Advanced data analysis can detect patterns in customer preferences in order to target the right customers with the right deal, at the right time. Unfortunately, the authors of the paper "Know What Your Customers Want Before They Do" see software as a substitute for the human connection. They write: "Today's distracted consumers, bombarded with information and options, often struggle to find the products or services that will best meet their needs. The short-handed and often poorly informed floor staff at many retailing sites can't begin to replicate the personal touch that shoppers once depended on and consumers are still largely on their own when they shop on-line."[27]

Of course that's a very pessimistic analysis of retail customer service. It suggests that retailers should give up on training all those "poorly informed floor staff" members and instead redirect their training and retention dollars into big data solutions.

Automation is used best when it supplements the staff, when it performs personalized tasks that would be impossible to achieve otherwise. For instance, the airline industry was one of the early adopters using automated text alerts to update passengers if a flight will be delayed. Now, Amtrak, UPS, Amazon, credit card companies, and many others employ similar text alerts. Companies that leverage text messaging as a way to communicate can also utilize it to answer more than the customer's question. A text alert can be sent with the same information the customer service agent provided, ensuring that the customers have any and all the information they need.

On the other hand, there is no automated substitute for most of our everyday customer interactions. For instance, before taking a business trip, I make a habit of contacting the hotel's concierge to recommend a car service. Over the years, I've found that I have a better customer experience if the driver is someone that the hotel staff knows and is willing to endorse.

This method is hardly foolproof, however. One such recommended driver met me at baggage claim, took me to his car, and drove me to the hotel without incident, but I was virtually ignored the entire trip. Because we had no connection, I never bothered to ask him for his name or number for my airport return or my next visit to the same city two months later. He, too, never offered any information about himself. With complete disinterest in me as a person, the driver and his company lost my business forever.

If frontline associates were trained to act more like tour guides, they would move customer service beyond providing efficient transactional assistance (which this driver did) and into the realm of building lasting connections. As strategic marketer Tom Smith points out, "Your customer-facing employees *are* your brand to many of your customers. They provide your products and services. They answer customer questions. They understand customers' needs and wants. They actually talk to your customer more than anyone else within your company . . . . While your actual brand is an inanimate, faceless company or corporation, the customer-facing employees are [the people] who your customers are developing an emotional connection to. And that's a good thing."

The Millennial challenge

The Millennial Generation—people born between 1980 and 1995—now represents the largest consumer group in the US population. According to a 2012 study, Millennials fundamentally tend to trust people over brands when making their purchase decisions. For instance, 84 percent say that user-generated content such as Yelp or TripAdvisor has at least some influence on what they buy.[28] These facts point to an urgent need on the part of companies to focus hiring and training on providing great and consistent customer service. You want your people to be the people Millennials trust with their purchases and rave about in social media.

"When it comes to serving Millennials, it all about personalization," says Guillermo Valiente of Tellus International. "They seek out only the information that's relevant for them. Millennials will want to know 'What's in it for me?'"[29] Your sales associates need to understand that if they want to connect with Millennials, this is where they are coming from.

It's important for companies to spell this out and hone in on specific product features that will meet their needs. As much as possible, communication with Millennials must be tailored to their individual tastes. Because Millennials are so eager to share what they like, including great customer experiences, it's vital for companies to provide engaging and compelling customer interactions.

Finally, it's just as important for companies to extend the customer experience over a period of time. Millennials have fewer dollars to spend than previous generations but are willing to spread out their spending over multiple paychecks. Smart companies will influence that future spending by training agents with both customer service and sales skills to offer incentives for Millennials to return. Research has shown that Millennials are the most likely group to pay for better service and do business with companies who are socially responsible.[30] This, coupled with their need for personalization, makes them the ideal candidates for creating a bond between a specific frontline associate and a customer. While Millennials may prefer electronic communication of texts or e-mails, there is still an opportunity to keep in touch using their preferred channel.

At Zappos, call center employees are carefully selected and trained to be fully empowered for the Millennial age. They don't work from a script. Their phone calls are not timed. They are encouraged to use their imaginations to make customers happy and provide a "wow" experience, without ever needing to ask for permission from a supervisor. Seventy-five percent of Zappos sales are from repeat customers, suggesting that the formula is working.

The best airline delay ever

Like many businesspeople, I spend more time waiting in airport lounges than I would like. One Friday at the Orlando airport, I assumed I would have a long wait before my flight to New York would depart. Delays are frequent on this busy corridor, and I knew the weather up north was iffy. But as I approached the gate, I saw that the aircraft was already there, offering a glimmer of hope.

The flight was supposed to depart at 3:25 p.m., with boarding to begin at 2:40. At two o'clock, however, the announcements began. The news wasn't good, but the customer service agent with the microphone spoke to all of us in the waiting area like personal friends, and he communicated bad news with a sense of humor, concern, empathy, and respect.

- His first words were, "I don't want to hear any moans before I finish everything I have to say." There were only laughs.

- He explained that the design of Newark airport makes it more challenging for air traffic controllers.

- He continued with a detailed explanation and tutorial on how poor visibility reduces the number of planes that can depart and land.

- He relayed that the pilot was in constant communication with Newark's air traffic control. The hope was that the flight would take off at 5:00 p.m. instead of 3:30, and his plans were to start the boarding process at 4:15, depart from the gate at 5:00, and be in the air at 5:30.

- He told the passengers they could leave the gate area, but it was important to check back every 20 minutes because that would be the amount of time to board if the flight was released earlier than expected.

- He explained that this flight was the next to Newark on any airline, so trying to switch flights would be a fruitless venture.

- He gave hope to passengers with connecting flights by saying that most likely all flights would be delayed and there was a good chance they might make theirs.

- He ended the announcement with a quiz. Yes, a quiz. He asked everyone to answer when the flight was boarding, being released from the gate, and taking off. Everyone shouted the answers. It was fun.

This airline employee did everything right. He educated everyone and provided us with additional useful information. He maintained confidence that he was in charge of the situation. In summary, he answered every question in advance. By answering every question, he not only communicated that he was in control but also gave every passenger a personal sense of control. With the information provided, each one of us could decide what was best.

Abhiroop Basu, content strategist for Zopim, a customer service software company, suggests these four handy ways to proactively engage your customers.

1. **Consider long-term loyalty**
   Build a relationship that demonstrates your awareness of each customer's information needs. Instead of sending out mass e-mails, try approaching each customer on an individual basis. For example, at Zopim they remind customers about new (and old) product features they may not have used. These reminders not only reinforce the brand message but also demonstrate that Zopim is paying attention to you, the customer.

2. **Use an ounce of prevention**
   Providing information and solutions to customers before they even know there's a problem is a great way to make them feel you're anticipating their needs, and it also reduces complaints in the form of support tickets. If a product shipment is going to be delayed, for instance, better to tell the customer now, instead of leaving the customer service team to deal with customer questions about where packages are.

3. **Answer questions before they are asked**
   Anticipating common questions and providing FAQs and guides can significantly increase sales. It is easy to come up with a list of questions commonly asked by potential customers; simply check with the CSRs and review support tickets.

4. **Put your reps in charge**
   At the end of the day, it is your CSR team that will interact with customers the most. So, instead of having them robotically answer questions, give them the leeway to delight your customers. Empowering your CSR team will increase their job satisfaction, commensurately increasing job retention and customer satisfaction.

Power Points Worth Repeating

- One-word answers are worse than inaccurate answers; they can mislead.

- Anticipating information customers didn't ask for builds trust and demonstrates competency.

- TCFCR's research has shown that 95 percent of customers are delighted when they are provided with additional useful information.

- By predicting the customer's needs, you are able to create an experience that is unique and special.

- Customers will ask more questions if invited.

- A returned item can become an opportunity to fortify a customer's loyalty or lose it entirely.

- It's critical for associates to be curious especially when the customer says, "I'm just looking."

- Instead of saying "I don't know," say "That's a good question; let me find out for you."

- Automation is best when it supplements the staff and assists in providing personalized service.

- Millennials fundamentally tend to trust people over brands when making purchasing decisions.

- For Millennials, it's all about personalization; they want to know "What's in it for me?"

- Millennials are the most likely group to pay for better service and do business with companies that are socially responsible.

- Keeping in touch with Millennials through their channel preferences shows them that their business is important.

4

Know Your Stuff

We live in Manhattan, not far from Macy's on 34th Street, the world's largest department store. We rarely shop there, but when a friend gave us a Macy's gift card at Christmas and we needed some new pillows, we decided to visit Macy's bedding and bath department.

So on a freezing cold morning in December, we met a sales associate on the sixth floor named Rochelle, who greeted us not only with a big smile but also like we were old friends. "I'm glad you're inside where it's warm. You must have something special in mind. How can I help?"

Rochelle asked us one good question after another about our furniture, our color scheme, and whether we had any photos. She also had many suggestions and knew the merchandise on the entire sixth floor like the back of her hand. She had a relationship with the other sales associates, too. It was a natural flow. Rochelle brought our choices to her register for us to consider so we didn't have to carry anything before we made our purchase.

We came for pillows and left with more. It was all because of Rochelle. She was eager to help and knew her stuff so well that she was extremely helpful. She gave us her e-mail address and said we could reach her anytime with questions. When we said our good-byes, we did leave as friends. We hadn't been to Macy's in years but knew we would shop there again.

The end of simple questions

There is no sales tool as powerful as knowledge. When we were shopping with Rochelle, we knew we were in good hands. Her expertise, coupled with a smile and an uplifting attitude, made all the difference.

If I go into a pet store, I expect the people working there to love animals. That makes sense to me. Taking care of dogs, cats, birds, and fish can be fun, but there are chores involved. Cleaning out a cage or bathing a dirty dog requires passion. When a pet store owner creates a profile for the perfect employee, being passionate about animals and being an excellent listener are prerequisites.

Similar thoughts go through my mind when I walk into a bookstore. I expect that a principal hiring practice for a sales associate would be a love of reading. I always ask the person behind the desk at Barnes & Noble what he or she has read recently and would recommend. How disappointing if the response was "Sorry, haven't read anything in the past year." Not the right fit for a bookseller.

Highly knowledgeable and discerning customer service is more important than ever today. Customers can get rudimentary questions answered online or on their phones. Shoppers are so proficient in gathering information that they don't need much guidance until they're just about ready to make their critical buying decisions. Maggie Fox, SAP's head digital marketer, estimates that marketing and communications messaging is now irrelevant for about 80 percent of the customer-decision journey.[31] As Fox might say, all sellers face this big question today: "Are your online resources and your staff up to the task of knowledgably responding to the questions remaining in that last 20 percent of the journey?"

Call center executives have noticed a somewhat similar changing dynamic in caller behavior. Agents are presented with increasingly complex issues to solve. Companies would benefit from updating their FAQs and information posted on social media to make sure that it is reflective of what the agents are responding to. Even the difficult questions and answers can be posted. Bottom line: all the matters that fall between the cracks wind up being handled by call center agents and sales associates.

The era of simple answers is over. We live in a complex society, and it takes a person with the ability to size up a customer's needs and match those needs with an appropriate service or product offering. It also requires more effective knowledgebase systems and quality monitoring processes that judge the quality of the call and not just the call time. Sales representatives of all kinds must be patient and understanding listeners, first and foremost, but they also must be solution-oriented problem solvers who know their stuff.

In 2012, automaker BMW started adding tech-savvy employees called "product geniuses" to their sales floors in Europe. The new workers, none of whom are commissioned salespeople, are trained in all the latest electronic features on new BMW models. They are experts and can explain and demonstrate how the car works to customers in a no-pressure environment. Sales of high-margin features climbed 10 to 15 percent in the dealerships that use product geniuses, and the program has since expanded to North America. "The product genius is not encumbered by the sale process and is not motivated to sell a car," BMW board member Ian Robertson told *Forbes*. "His motivation is customer satisfaction."[32]

There are 20,000 BMW salespeople worldwide, and some are going to be replaced by product geniuses, a new breed of employee. One large BMW dealership has stated plans to shift away from its current ratio of one genius to four salespeople and increase the number of geniuses so there are more of them than salespeople.

Robertson says that many BMW geniuses are young and recruited directly from universities. "Some came from airlines, from the service industry, from [retail] environments. This works because what we're looking for is that customer empathy, as well as the ability to use the digital tools that we have."[33]

The BMW approach, borrowed from Apple's "genius bar" retail concept, is now being copied by other carmakers, including Lexus and Cadillac. The trend reflects the fact that customers want someone who is trained and knowledgeable about a company's merchandise and its service offerings. Customers expect to speak to a person who either knows the answer to their question immediately or has easy access to information and can provide a quick reply. This is accomplished through websites and knowledgebase systems even for the salesperson or genius. They understand what they're looking for—further evidence that they know their stuff.

BMW's cutting-edge investment in customer satisfaction reflects its ranking near the top in the auto industry when it comes to brand loyalty. When customers get their complex questions answered and intricate problems resolved, they remember. Many will take the time to post positive comments on social media sites and become the most loyal brand advocates. When I contemplate the meaning of loyalty and what drives it, I think about people—not places, not stores, not even brands. I think of people who know their merchandise and also know me well enough to guide me toward what's best for me.

For many companies, the point of initial contact, when the phone rings or the customer walks into a store or visits a website, the issue the customer has will be the one that impacts whether the relationship with the brand is renewed or diminished. We never used to think of Macy's, and now if we need something new for our bedroom or bath, that's the only store we think of, because Rochelle is there. When we wanted new towels, Rochelle got an e-mail with a request for her hours so she could help us. We were looking forward to seeing her again.

Employee retention

Rochelle has been working at Macy's for many years. Her thorough knowledge of the sixth-floor merchandise has been seasoned with time and experience. In order to be a trusted guide for the customer, it's not always enough to be welcoming, engaging, and curious. A sales associate who has been on the job for only a short time will find it difficult, if not impossible, to deliver the ultimate customer service experience. Knowledge and expertise build with time and experience.

Most jobs in retail, however, are part-time, and annual turnover in the field is often more than 60 percent. Large call centers report a 50 percent turnover for a third of their departments.[34] Other service industries, such as banking and hospitality, also have churn rates, despite their heavy dependence on frontline associates to help build loyalty among customers.

Turnover creates two basic problems for the consumer. First, it means that most associates are neither experienced nor knowledgeable enough to really deliver the brand experience. Then, when a good sales associate is found, there's not much chance he or she will still be around in a few months when you return. In my first book I told the story of how I used to shop for clothes exclusively at a Nordstrom store near my office because of Ruth in the men's furnishings department. She was the ultimate sales professional. Ruth was attentive and understood my needs, and whenever I wanted or needed to add to my wardrobe, I would call her for an appointment. Then she moved. My next visit to Nordstrom was my last. The store had enjoyed my loyalty and my dollars for many years, but lost it when it lost Ruth.

What could Nordstrom have done differently? Perhaps the company policy could have instructed sales associates who may be transferring to other locations to arrange for an introductory meeting with an associate whom they feel would be a good fit for their customers. Such a meeting would benefit everyone in this case since I had no desire to stop going to Nordstrom and Nordstrom presumably would have preferred not to lose a loyal customer.

When compensation consultants calculate the cost of employee turnover, they use estimates that range from 15 to over 150 percent of the annual salary for a given position. Many direct costs go into this equation, such as the expense of ad placement, search firms, candidate testing, and hours spent reviewing applications. The indirect costs include loss of productivity and the time and expense involved in skills training.

And yet, in a retail environment, I believe that the greatest cost of employee turnover is the one that is rarely quantified or even discussed: the diminished staff capacity in terms of customer relationships and institutional knowledge. With inexperienced staff, customers might very well have a good purchasing experience if their sales associate was welcoming and engaging. But those same customers may not return in the future, nonetheless, if they feel what they really need is someone with an in-depth grasp of the store's merchandise.

While the true cost of turnover in this sense may be difficult or even impossible to calculate, there needs to be a greater appreciation of how frontline employees help generate revenue for the company—and how revenue is lost when a high-turnover location gets a reputation for having an inexperienced staff.

Kip Tindell, CEO of The Container Store, a home-organization retailer, says that one great sales associate can be as productive and beneficial to the bottom line as three ordinary associates. This "one equals three" equation is a foundational principle of the Store's hiring practices, and it justifies why some employees there are paid 50 to 100 percent above the industry average.[35]

Here are a few other unusual personnel practices at The Container Store:

- **Reward successful entry-level associates**—Entry-level associates are reviewed and given increases after the first three months. While everyone appreciates a salary bump, Tindell says getting a raise when first starting a career is a great motivator. It's another way that The Container Store attracts good people to apply for positions within the company.

- **Provide quality feedback**—Employees are reviewed on an annual basis, and their managers spend four or five hours not only providing feedback but also discussing each of the performance criteria in detail. This allows the manager and employee to study the overall assessment and create improvement plans that work.

- **Encourage employees to recommend job applicants**—The Container Store does not rely on human resources for the applicant pool but encourages current associates to recommend individuals they know. Associates at The Container Store may suggest interviewing a friend who would be a good fit for the company or perhaps a waiter they had who showed great customer service skills during a recent restaurant visit. There are no rules against hiring relatives at The Container Store, and Tindell's wife, Sharon, is his chief merchandising officer.

- **Keep the superstars**—In The Container Store paradigm, employees are given large annual increases based on their individual contributions. In other words, they are rewarded based on their ROI. With services and products becoming so much more complex, consumers relish experience and want to interact with confident frontline associates.

- **Maintain your principles during good times and bad**—When asked about a recent stock price decline, Tindell says that employee pay rates are part of the company's business model and shouldn't be compromised due to fluctuations and bumps in the road. Doing what a company believes is right is the constant.

Built into The Container Store's approach is the acknowledgment that products and services are becoming more complicated. Having frontline associates who are product experts makes it easier to deliver a superior customer experience. It takes time for associates to learn about your company's specific policies, procedures, and all the technical nuances. In order to truly estimate the cost of high turnover in your employee ranks, you should include the cost of losing customers, especially when you have frontline associates who are dedicated, deliver superior customer service, and are connected to store patrons.

When our company conducted a benchmarking study of call center employees, we discovered that most associates don't feel that their employers are properly focused on how they can best serve customers. For instance, associates said they felt that contact center management put a greater stress on reducing average call durations instead of measuring customer satisfaction—a metric that addresses the actual quality of the call.

We found that most associates really do care. They are loyal to the company and want to provide quality service to consumers. Getting the associates more involved with how their roles impact the brand will make them feel more valued. Additionally, having the associates become an integral part of the training and coaching process will ultimately enable them to deliver better customer service.

The same study found that slightly less than 50 percent of the respondents envisioned working in a contact center environment to be their career. Therefore, it's important for management to create career paths so representatives feel more committed to the brands and the companies they represent.

In too many industries—fast food, retail, and contact centers among them—management fails to see the connection between keeping good associates and bottom-line profitability. But there are signs that this is changing. Inspired by the example of Costco, which pays employees above its industry's average and still keeps prices low, "fast-casual" restaurants such as Chipotle and Shake Shack are setting themselves apart by offering better food, better service, better customer experiences, and higher pay in order to retain employees.

"The number one reason we pay our team well above the minimum wage is because we believe that if we take care of the team, they will take care of our customers," Randy Garutti, the chief executive of Shake Shack told *The New York Times*.[36] Shake Shack, Chipotle, and others have broken with the conventional wisdom in the fast-food industry of keeping employee expenses at the absolute minimum, as if the customer experience doesn't matter. Fast food stocks have been in the doldrums for more than a decade, while Chipotle's stock grew 2,865 percent between its initial public offering in 2006 and 2014.[37] Shake Shack launched a hot initial public offering in early 2015.[38]

One of the components of reducing turnover and increasing associate knowledge is providing consistency in the work schedule. Certain companies maintain tenure in retail environments by ensuring that their full-time associates always work the same schedule throughout the year. This makes it much easier to plan for childcare or to take care of a sick relative. Employers who make a practice of sending people home with little notice due to unexpectedly light customer traffic will never be able to attract top employees (and some states now forbid the practice). Providing regular schedules, like fair pay, is a simple matter of treating associates with respect, which benefits both the company and the employees.

The connection between higher worker pay and higher profits is not that new an idea. In 1914, Henry Ford more than doubled the daily wages for unskilled workers in his factories from $2.34 to $5.00. In today's dollars, that's the equivalent of raising wages from $6.93 to $14.80 per hour (well above Michigan's current minimum wage of $8.15 per hour).

At the time, other prominent businesspeople thought Ford was crazy, and they were angry that he'd disrupted what had been considered a "fair" daily wage. But Ford's factories had been plagued with excessive absenteeism and turnover rates of a staggering 370 percent.[39] The factory jobs were monotonous, and it was too easy for employees to find better alternatives. Offering higher wages made Ford jobs more valuable, more desirable, and more attractive to people who had other choices—the exact kind of people Ford wanted to attract. The result was increased morale, lower employee turnover, and, most importantly, significantly improved productivity.

One hundred years later, many businesses continue to ignore the lessons of Henry Ford and others. Keeping valuable employees on your company's payroll is one of the best investments you can make, one that provides an excellent ROI. But when your customer-friendly, knowledgeable, and reliable associates leave your organization and go to your competitor, you've lost twice.

Training and selection

For your workers to provide customers with truly valuable guidance, your company needs to support them in that effort. Every business has the capability of hiring representatives who are more welcoming, more engaging, and more interested in seeing the customer as a person first and a customer second. A specific representative at one of your check-out counters, a telephone associate, or your afternoon receptionist may be responsible for more repeat business than others. Make sure that every day you consider the dollar value of each associate before those associates leave and go to work for someone else.

The nature of customer service is changing, and so is the nature of hiring and retention. In the words of LinkedIn founder Reid Hoffman, there is now a new unspoken contract between employers and employees, one that's more of an "alliance," he says. For individual workers, this new alliance requires giving up the old idea of lifetime employment and instead seeking out employers who offer "lifetime employability." Workers should find companies willing to invest in them by offering more training and expanded responsibilities. In exchange, he says the employees "will work to keep the company adapting and valuable and growing over the long term."[40]

Hoffman's point is that highly adaptive employees can keep companies vibrant, and they are also much more likely to stay and thrive in an environment where they are always learning new things and being challenged. Again, this is not a totally new idea. My experience in the corporate world taught me long ago that it made sense to hire smart people and continue to give them responsibility so they had opportunities to grow. Providing financial incentives and allowing time to pursue higher education also contribute to company loyalty.

Here are my six top ways to prevent your most valued employees from seeking work elsewhere (and prevent other companies from poaching your best people):

1. **Encourage associates to take on additional responsibility**—Tell company associates to take on additional responsibilities. This will help the company and the employees feel more invigorated. But this cannot be accomplished in an environment where everyone is overworked. Having a platform of work-life balance will facilitate people wanting to learn and do more to keep themselves challenged and their minds fresh. Scott Newman, a manager at the Boloco's restaurant chain, says, "When you teach talented individuals, once they get it, they'll be a rock star for you."[41]

2. **Assign them to visit other locations**—Ensure that your associates don't work in a vacuum. Have managers visit various company locations to meet with others who do the same type of job. It's one of the best ways to learn. It opened up an entire new

world for me when I worked in a highly structured corporate environment.

3. **Help them continue their educations**—Encourage your employees to seek additional college and advanced degree courses. Bring in "Lunch and Learn" speakers on various subjects. Find internal associates who have become experts in their field to give periodic courses to their fellow associates. It could be workshops on exercise, nutrition, travel, six sigma, etc.

4. **Support them in their efforts with volunteering or charity work**—There is no better way to network and help others along the way than by giving back to those less fortunate. In general, people who like to help also make the best service-oriented thinkers. Those who give of themselves make their own rewards.

5. **Allow them to make mistakes**—The only way to grow personally and business-wise is to make mistakes. Albert Einstein said, "Anyone who has never made a mistake has never tried anything new." If people are afraid of what can go wrong, a level of greatness can never be achieved to give your company a competitive edge.

6. **Involve them in your successes and setbacks**—Share results with your staff. Let them see how your department is performing against others within the company. Competitive spirit works great in sports, and it can work even more effectively in a business environment. Sometimes the devil is in the details, and having staff focused will help uncover new opportunities for success.

Treat your employees as you would your best customers and make them feel valued. Compensate them fairly. Provide them with the utmost respect. Ensure that company employees have the most prolific LinkedIn profiles based on their robust experience. This might make them prey for your competitors. But, as Hoffman would suggest, your staff will appreciate how you have taught and coached them over the years and will think more than twice about leaving an environment where their contributions have been welcomed.

Company-wide competence

Sometimes when I discover a very special frontline employee who is exceptionally helpful and knowledgeable, I seek out that person's manager to communicate my delight. In most cases, the managers respond with indifference, as though my opinion doesn't matter. Others even react with arrogance, as though my comments are some kind of unwelcome meddling. Negative responses of these kinds tell me that the special employee is succeeding in *spite* of that company's culture, not because of it.

Nordstrom is famous for its company culture and because of it is able to empower employees to do what they think is best for the customer. For a long time, it was rumored that Nordstrom's employee handbook consisted of one line, "Use your best judgment in all situations. There will be no additional rules." Nordstrom's customer service standards are strong enough to support its employees, who in turn are empowered to help Nordstrom's customers.

It's at the critical moments, when a judgment must be made, that your company's customer service standards, practices, and training are put to the test. A Bain and Company survey showed that banking customers prefer standing in line for a teller only at times when online banking and ATMs don't suit their needs. These usually highly important make-or-break moments—such as replacing a lost credit card, processing an urgent payment, or just getting a receipt for a deposit—are when customers crave personal connections. That's also when the customer's perception of your business and your brand is most heavily influenced.

Contact center associates are the face and voice of a company, which also means that in the long run, they can't be much better than the company's culture. It is important for them to be strong brand advocates, feel good about their career path, and be evaluated on their effectiveness in building customer relationships. There is a chain of mutual respect and appreciation that extends up and down the customer journey. Customers appreciate associates that appreciate them. At the same time, associates appreciate management that appreciates their role in the company and provides the appropriate support.

There are two other important points we discovered in that call center benchmarking survey I noted in a previous segment of this chapter. First, while most representatives felt some kind of connection to the brand, tremendous opportunities exist to increase that connection. Associates appreciate being educated about the history of their brands. They like having additional insights into the production and distribution facilities on which their jobs rely. Involving associates whenever possible in your competitive market research will also increase their connection and awareness of your brand and company's position.

The other important point is that communication within contact centers is almost always lacking and in need of improvement. One of the key goals of any improved communication strategy should be to make sure associates understand their roles as being important to the success of the company. Associates grow frustrated and alienated when they are not notified about new products, special product promotions, and other initiatives that have an impact on customers. So often when a consumer poses a question or concern that is unfamiliar to a call center associate, it's because marketing failed to tell the call center about some new change or promotion. The marketing department should have a direct connection with the frontline people who are talking to their customers every day. It's wrong to leave those people out of the loop.

It all comes down to a challenge of competence that the entire company must address. Research has shown that the more connected a representative is to the brand he or she represents, the greater the probability is that he or she will be able to effectively communicate with current and potential customers about the product's benefits and features. But a sales associate cannot cover for incompetence in other aspects of the customer journey.

In 2014, revenues increased by an average of 22.2 percent for the Fortune 100 Best Companies to Work For. And according to the Bureau of Labor Statistics, these same companies added new employees at a rate that was five times higher than the national average.[42] Some of the reasons that were mentioned why employees were happy included:

- Pay fairly

- Provide awesome benefits

- Keep an open leadership door—and an open mind

- Share the profits

- Make sure the workplace is fun

One of my favorite stories about these companies involves Chicago-based Radio Flyer, which ranked thirteenth on the *Fortune* list.

The company has been making toy wagons and, as it says, creating fond childhood memories for people since it was founded in 1917. Almost 100 years later, employees appreciate that Radio Flyer is a fun and family-like place to work. The ingrained sense of teamwork and family makes Radio Flyer special. The CEO, Robert Pasin—known as the "chief wagon officer"—personally meets with all candidates, and some new hires get one of the company's iconic wagons filled with flowers delivered to their home before the first day. Nine out of 10 employees say their work has special meaning and that it's not just a job.[43]

I worry about the future of retailing when I see sales associates for whom the work is just a job, with no special meaning. The Millennial Generation has grown up in an e-commerce heaven, and brick-and-mortar retail shops are in deep trouble if they can't offer this up-and-coming generation the special experiences they crave.

One of our friend's daughters, Kathi, recently ordered 20 dresses from Bloomingdales online. That may sound crazy, but thanks to Bloomingdale's indulgent return policy, it made perfect sense. She tried on all 20 dresses in the comfort and privacy of her home and sent 19 of them back to the store for a full refund. Can Bloomingdales possibly make money on customers who behave like this? I truly doubt it.

I wonder what would happen if Kathi happened to walk into Bloomingdales one day and found someone to help her, like my Ruth from Nordstrom or our Rochelle from Macy's. I would imagine that either one of these experienced and knowledgeable salespeople would get to know Kathi's needs, her likes, or her style and what outfits looked best on her. It would probably be a better, more satisfying experience for Kathi, and it would certainly be the same for Bloomingdale's.

Power Points Worth Repeating

- It's important for associates to be passionate and excellent listeners.

- The era of simple answers is over.

- When customers get their complex questions answered or problems resolved, they remember.

- Loyalty is generally connected to another person, not to places, stores, or even brands.

- The initial contact for any channel can either renew or diminish the customer relationship.

- Getting associates involved with the brand will make them feel more valued.

- In too many industries, management fails to see the connection between retaining good associates and bottom-line profitability.

- Managers who send associates home with little notice will not attract top candidates.

- Customers appreciate associates who appreciate them.

5

Don't Tell Me No

I was standing in line at a Staples store when the customer in front of me asked the cashier about her Staples reward account. She had signed up several months earlier and wondered why she wasn't receiving discounts. The cashier, certainly professional and polite, told the customer that maybe she had not accumulated enough points to trigger a savings coupon.

The customer gave a compliant "OK," but anyone could see she wasn't happy. The associate, though pleasant, was noncommittal. She had no interest in helping the customer solve the riddle of her account. The cashier basically said, "I don't know, and I don't care."

When I suggest, in the previous chapter, that associates should know their stuff, it's not a command that every employee be a walking encyclopedia of knowledge about the company. There are limits to what anyone can be expected to know about anything and everything your company offers. But there is no limit to respect and looking out for the needs of the customer. "I don't know" is forgivable only if there is a clear intention that you care and will do your best to get an answer.

What else might the cashier have done? She could have advised the customer to check her Staples reward account on the web. Or she might have taken the customer's e-mail address and offered to forward it to customer service. If the customer isn't receiving discounts, perhaps there is a problem with her account. Maybe the application had not been processed or the customer's address was entered incorrectly. Any discussion of these problems and responses would be acceptable. Every question from a customer provides an opportunity for engagement and the possibility of helping the customer get what he or she wanted. Every frontline associate must understand that being respectful to the customer is exactly what is expected and required whenever a question exposes a gap in that associate's knowledge.

There are so many different ways to say no. One of the most popular is "I don't know." Others include "I can't," "We're not allowed," and "The system won't let me." None of these phrases should ever be said. Such flat refusals will always leave a customer with a negative memory of the experience (see sidebar) and a good reason never to return. It's impossible to say how many customers are lost forever in such exchanges. One thing is certain, though. Whatever goodwill your staff might build with customers by excelling at the first four principles in this book, it will be utterly wasted if they fail to learn the art of avoiding the word "no."

Offering choices

Whenever someone asks whether we know a good contractor, we immediately and without hesitation forward the contact information for Michael. He is the very skilled professional who renovated our apartment in Manhattan. The project took months to complete and was filled with the issues you might expect to encounter working in a 50-year-old building. But Michael has earned our everlasting gratitude and respect because of the way he handled everything. He always presented problems to us in terms of possible solutions. We didn't always get what we wanted, but he never told us no.

Michael would say, "We have a problem, but don't worry. I have two solutions, and you get to choose which one you prefer." The options were not always ideal, but like anyone, we appreciated that he was offering us a choice. "One option might cost a bit more," Michael would say, "and the other might take more time." Decisions were always in our hands. Michael offered us that sense of control that all customers value and paved the way to a successful completion.

Creating solutions—instead of saying "no," "can't," or "won't"—takes time, effort, and often some imagination. But it's worth it. By developing problem-solving ideas and then communicating the issue in terms of options, you reduce the anxiety that arises when the ideal solution isn't available. Of course the same is true in the business world. How many executives communicate to their employees about problems in terms of "can't" and "won't"? Sales associates are not trained to do what comes naturally to Michael, our contractor: think first and offer possible solutions. If associates are trained this way, you're less likely to lose dissatisfied customers and more likely to increase your positive reviews on social media sites.

Let's say it's August and a customer wants to buy gloves for an upcoming trip to Alaska. You can apologize sincerely and express with confidence that gloves will arrive during the third week of September. This response certainly satisfies the need to answer more than the customer's question. On the other hand, it also tells the customer "no" and "good-bye."

A better response is "I can help you with that," followed by these small but important gestures. You can offer to speak with your manager and arrange to special order the gloves. Or you can ask the manager to contact the manufacturer to find out specifically what gloves are coming in and when or whether they will be preordered. In any case, you can give the customer options and offer to get back to him or her ASAP however is most convenient: e-mail, text, or phone call.

The result is that you have created an opportunity to form a relationship in a situation where you could not satisfy the customer's direct request. You have the customer's contact information, and you know the type of merchandise the customer is looking for. Even if the customer prefers to look for gloves elsewhere, the interaction was memorable because the customer was not sent away; in fact, the opposite occurred. That's the reason why when you can't say yes, you nonetheless must never say no.

In some cases, the item you are looking for may be available only online and not in a store. Sometimes, Target and Best Buy offer the opportunity to buy online and have it delivered to the store. But what if you're in the store looking for the gloves and the salesperson tells you the store doesn't have it and you can only get it online? Another missed opportunity. Companies should simplify the shopping experience for their customers by making items available where they want them. That doesn't mean keeping an endless inventory, but it does mean that the technology must be in place to allow associates to order something for a customer and the policies in place so they don't have to say no.

The word "no" is never necessary because you should always tell customers what you can do, not what you can't do. When the rules and policies don't allow you to fulfill their wishes or when you're out of stock and unable to ship sooner or make a substitution, you can still offer alternative options (including checking with a competitor). Use your imagination and offer direction as to how their needs might be fulfilled in other ways. And check and double-check to make sure that your inclination to tell them "no" isn't just the lazy way out.

Every communication with customers should invite a reply. For instance, when you register with a new e-commerce site, you typically get an immediate e-mail confirmation, a golden opportunity for the company to welcome and engage you. Instead, the subject line on most such e-mails is "DO NOT REPLY." I also see this "DO NOT REPLY" message when I e-mail a company with a question and receive an auto-reply confirmation. Big mistake. What they should do is tell me how else I can get in touch if I need additional information. They could offer the option of a number to call or a link to an FAQ site or social media. But simply telling someone not to reply is tantamount to telling him or her that what he or she has to say just doesn't interest you. Again, a missed opportunity to create and build a relationship.

Never saying no is all about trying your best, because people will always come back to do business with a company that gives them the feeling that it is there for you. Shep Hyken, author of *The Amazement Revolution*, tells of a retailer he knows that will send a customer to a competitor but only after the retailer calls the competitor, makes sure the item is in stock, and has it held in the customer's name. "Most of the time, the customers are appreciative, seeing that the store is more interested in taking care of the customer than making a sale," Hyken writes. "In the long term, the store gains the customer's loyalty and trust."[44]

If you are truly determined never to say no, sometimes there can be unexpected benefits even beyond preserving one customer relationship and loyalty. A Brooklyn courier service company made it a part of company culture to never say no to customers or coworkers. So when a call came in asking whether the company provided document storage space, the associate on the phone didn't say no, even though that was the truth. He took down the caller's information and passed it onto the company owner, Norm Brodsky.

The inquiry made Brodsky curious about the document storage business. He did some research and discovered that document storage rates were so high that he could easily rent some warehouse space and use his fleet of courier trucks to pick up and deliver documents from the warehouse. He was perfectly positioned to enter a profitable and fast-growing line of business but never realized it until he got that message. Years later, Brodsky spun off his company's highly successful document storage business for $110 million—all because his company's culture was to never say no.[45]

Mistakes happen

In any business, there are going to be errors and mishaps. A defective product might have shipped, or customer response either is handled poorly or is not what the customer expected. When that happens, it's a resounding way of saying no, because the customer's expectations are thwarted at the very moment those expectations are at their peak.

Customer disappointment and distress must be handled with the same single objective with which you do everything—to preserve the customer relationship. When you put the customer relationship first, you can see that every error and every screwup provide a company with a unique opportunity to shine. As the old saying goes, success is determined not by how you fall down but by how you get up.

Ingrid Lindberg, customer experience officer at the healthcare insurer Cigna, tells the story of a woman who was so angered by Cigna's automated call system that she went on Twitter to threaten physical violence against the company. Within hours, Cigna's social media team had invited the aggrieved woman into a private online chat forum and worked with her to make sure the calls would stop. The woman was so delighted by Cigna's responsiveness that she sent a tweet the very same day volunteering to be "president of the Cigna fan club." The speedy response was what is expected from a healthcare insurer, Lindberg said. "We help people beat cancer, lose hundreds of pounds; we change people's lives," she pointed out. "Being able to solve someone's issues that quickly is critical."[46] The anger and frustration in the customer's initial message did not deter Lindberg from making a human connection.

When automated response systems do not offer customers a user-friendly experience and one that allows them to easily reach a live agent, the company is communicating a message of no. A 2006 *New York Times* article, "Your Call Should Be Important to Us, but It's Not," described Paul English's company, GetHuman.com. He shared the secret code, a cheat sheet, for reaching a live agent at various large companies. GetHuman was created because of customer frustration. Almost 10 years later, companies don't understand that forcing your customers to only self-serve has the potential to destroy customer loyalty.

No one likes to deal with angry people, not in his or her personal life and not as a frontline associate. While most customers realize that you, the associate, are not personally at fault, you do represent the company and often bear the brunt of the negativity. So what are some of the best ways to diffuse a negative situation?

Here are some suggestions for not only showing customers that you are ready to help them with their issue but also creating loyalty along the way:

- **Listen for the underlying emotion**—Always listen; this has already been explored but is worth repeating. Every unhappy customer has a specific emotion. The customer could be feeling sad, angry, frustrated, or furious. Listening and acknowledging the emotional root of the customer's unhappiness are the first steps in demonstrating that you actually "hear" him or her.

- **Reflect the emotion**—After determining the underlying emotion, say, "I hear you are frustrated, but I want to help you with your problem." This will almost immediately calm the customer. If you haven't heard the correct emotion, the consumer will let you know. "I'm not frustrated; I'm really disappointed in the store's policies. I have been a customer for years and am being treated terribly." At that point, you can set the stage for a more cordial exchange by acknowledging the feeling of disappointment.

- **Use the word "help"**—Saying throughout the conversation, "I would like to help you with that," "I'm so glad you are here (or called) so I can help you," or "You have come to the right place (or person) for help" will send a strong message to the customer that you really do want to do just that—help.

- **Be flexible**—Rules should be guidelines, not rigid policies that cannot be adjusted. Is it really worth losing a loyal customer who might spend $500 or more a year over a $25 dispute?

- **Be empowered**—Make sure that company policies empower the frontline associates to make decisions regarding customer satisfaction, without a manager's consent. Having a dollar amount that can instantly make a customer happy and loyal is a powerful tool when addressing customer complaints. When associates have little or no authority, it reflects poorly on the organization and does nothing to create long-lasting customer relationships. The company must empower the employee.

- **Personalize the conversation**—Be observant. Compliment the customer on something he or she is wearing or ask how his or her day is going. As long as it doesn't sound like you're trying to change the subject, engaging the customer and assuring that you see him or her as a person, not just trouble, is powerful.

Apologies have been proven to make people *more* loyal than before they got angry—but only if the apologies are handled correctly. Most of us, whether we are in the customer service industry or not, have little tolerance for bad service. I know I can get angry and frustrated by robotic, indifferent, or hostile service associates and unfriendly customer policies. But, I also know that if a representative is responsive to my emotions and offers help, I have a normal human need to repay the favor. I'm eager to put a smile back on my face, be cooperative, and allow help to come my way.

Here's an important point of caution. Remedies are dependent on what went wrong. If someone feels that he or she was treated rudely, that person wants a sincere apology. But if work was done wrong, it should be fixed or the customer given compensation. If you try to compensate someone for rude treatment or merely apologize for a bad outcome, you compound the grievance because you're not paying attention.

In 2011, Airbnb, the fast-growing Web company that is a source for short-term home and apartment stays, generated a torrent of bad press by telling a wronged customer a big no. An Airbnb subscriber had vandalized and ransacked another subscriber's apartment, and Airbnb rejected the customer's request for compensation by citing its fine-print policy of not insuring against damages or losses. It took a firestorm of negative media attention and online chatter (thanks to the customer's blog and Twitter complaints) before Airbnb relented and compensated the customer for thousands of dollars' worth of damage.

The experience taught Airbnb executives a valuable lesson. No is never an acceptable answer. As a result, the company totally revamped its policies and staffing. Customer support staff was doubled and a 24-hour customer hotline opened, and there is now a $50,000 liability guarantee for property owners. When another incident of gross vandalism happened in New York in 2014, within hours of receiving the report, Airbnb wired the wronged customer more than $23,000 in compensation, dispatched a locksmith to secure the premises, and put the customer in a hotel while repairs were made.

Airbnb then received great press for its "almost absurdly swift response" to this one customer's calamity. Even in the face of disastrous circumstances, Airbnb had prompted a systematic reorientation toward total customer satisfaction, all because of one terrible experience with saying no.[47]

Company executives too often miss the forest for the trees. They say their employees should "think outside the box" but don't create the path to do just that. Too many times employees are afraid to make a mistake, hide a mistake, or take any risk to improve the customer experience and earn customer loyalty. Employees fear retribution because of a mistake. Fear creates an environment of stagnation instead of motivation.

The number one rule at my grandson's summer camp is "Don't be afraid to make a mistake." Camp Winadu's 90-year anniversary is just around the corner, so it must be doing something right. Its mission is "Building Character through Sports," and through their programs, children learn critical life lessons while having lots of fun.

Some of those lessons are:

- Win with humility.

- Lose with pride in your efforts.

- Be good teammates.

- Respect your opponents.

- Take care of your bodies.

- Value cooperation.

- Value consistent, sustained effort.

Camp Winadu believes that "children learn best in an environment where they are encouraged to try new things and improve their abilities without fear of criticism." This is how one builds character, that distinctive quality in an individual's life that determines his or her response regardless of circumstances.

Take the above statement and replace the word "children" with "people." I think there are many corporate leaders who would do well to spend some time at Camp Winadu. They might learn to create a business culture in which employees would be encouraged to overcome fear of mistakes, behave like cooperative teammates, and value consistent, sustained effort. Any company with that kind of culture is a company that creates loyalty.

Beyond apologies

Sometimes with customer complaints, your efforts to fix things won't bear fruit. If you can find no practical resolution or if one is not warranted, I have found that an about-face is in order. Simply ask the customer what he or she would do in this particular situation if he or she managed or owned the business. Such a suggestion returns to the customer that all-important feeling of control. It also produces a concrete structure for negotiating a solution and may even provide various options not yet considered.

Once a conflict has been resolved, it's a good idea to call or write to the customer a day or two after the problem has been rectified, just to check whether everything is still OK. Such a gesture can go a long way toward healing the relationship if it suffered some bruises from whatever trouble was encountered. Too many businesses look at customer transactions in a vacuum instead of thinking about the lifetime value. Acknowledging past loyalty communicates appreciation and will pave the way toward restoring the relationship—especially when it comes to an angry customer.

A 2013 national "Customer Rage Study" documented how customers aren't getting this kind of care at all when things go wrong. Among customers with complaints, the most common need expressed is "to be treated with dignity." Ninety-four percent said they wanted that, but only 35 percent said they got it. Seventy-two percent said that a sincere apology would have made them happy following a negative experience, but only 32 percent said they received any kind of apology.

Interestingly, some form of compensation or refund was desired by less than half. Most wanted a sincere apology and the assurance that it would not happen again. (Eighty percent of survey respondents expressed the desire to be thanked for their business, but only 33 percent said they were.[48])

Ultimately, the best way to avoid apologizing to customers is obviously to avoid making them upset in the first place. Unfortunately, many companies have standard practices that needlessly leave their customers feeling disappointed and uncared for. For instance, our firm conducted a comprehensive customer satisfaction survey for a cosmetic products company and found an inventory practice that was an ongoing source of severe customer dismay. Whenever the company discontinued a product, such as a particular shade of lipstick, the procedure was to immediately ship all remaining units to outlet stores, where they would be sold at a discount.

Our survey revealed that a number of unhappy customers were calling to complain they could no longer find their favorite lipstick shade. The call center was never provided information about newly discontinued products, so the associates had to tell the unhappy customers they couldn't help them. Remember for a moment these are customers who love the company products so much they've gone to the trouble to call. And company procedure was to tell these loyal customers no.

Once we provided our analysis and this problem had been identified, the fix was remarkably simple. The company changed its procedure so that a portion of all discontinued items were to be set aside for distribution upon request by the consumer affairs department. That one simple change gave customer service associates at long last a way to say yes to those aggrieved customers. The associates were also educated as to newer colors that might be a very close substitution for the discontinued products, thus offering the customer choice and the feeling of control. By letting customers know that their frustration is heard and that they can special order their favorite product and might also want to try a new alternative, the customer affairs department gave loyal patrons the opportunity to remain loyal.

Exercising this kind of thoughtfulness, by saying yes when the answer is usually no, has earned valuable media attention for some companies. In 2013, the parents of a five-year-old Atlanta girl were upset when they found out that McCormick's had discontinued their daughter's favorite spice, Mediterranean Herb. That was the spice mix the family used to cook fish, one of the few foods their daughter would eat. The parents sent an e-mail to McCormick's CEO, but instead of passing the query along to consumer affairs, the CEO's office responded the same day with a promise to help. Within a week, they had shipped a free case of the beloved spice to the family. The parents shared the story with the press because they felt it clearly demonstrated that McCormick cares about its customers. A potential no became a public relations and social media win for the company.[49]

Social media makes the stakes very high when it comes to handling complaints correctly. Saying no can exact a heavy toll far beyond the hurt feelings of the single customer being denied. The most famous case is that of Dave Carroll, a professional musician who wanted United Airlines to compensate him $1,200 for damaging his guitar. United Airlines told Carroll no many times and in a variety of ways. Airline employees told him there must have been something wrong with his guitar case, cited a damage waiver he'd signed, and then told him he'd waited too long to file his claim.

After eight months of pleading with United's customer service officials, he received an e-mail message that was unambiguous. The subject heading was "The Final No!" In the body of the message, the United representative wrote she would no longer respond to any of Carroll's future e-mails. That's really the ultimate no, isn't it? United Airlines customer service all but told Mike Carroll that he was dead to them.

So Carroll communicated in the way he knew best. He wrote and recorded a catchy song called "United Breaks Guitars" and then posted it on YouTube. Four days later, it had been seen all over the world more than one million times, and United's stock price tumbled by 10 percent.[50]

Only then did United offer to pay for Dave Carroll's broken guitar—but with the condition that he remove "United Breaks Guitars" from YouTube.

Can you guess what he told United?

No.[51]

Childhood Memories of No

For most of us, "no" is a trigger that sets in motion an entire chain of negative emotions. Anger, outrage, argumentation. These are all baked into our DNA. Somewhere between your sixth and twelfth month of life, you first made a realization that has stuck with you until this day:

If Mommy says no, you have three options:

- Accept it and move on (unlikely).
- Go ask Daddy (since you've still got a 50/50 shot of getting a yes from him).
- Kick and scream to show your displeasure, hoping your outburst will change the no into a yes.

In a service interaction, when most customers hear no, they do one of a number of things—all of which are pretty bad outcomes for the company (and not all that different from how we responded when we were children):

- Engage in some emotional response. Argue with the rep, get angry, use foul language, create some kind of outburst.
- Hang up, call back, and try again with another rep, often called "rep shopping." This, of course, is the customer version of the "Go ask Daddy" reaction.

- Escalate the call. By asking the rep to transfer you to his or her supervisor, you're playing a more savvy version of the rep-shopping game, since most customers have learned that the supervisor has more authority to waive annoying fees, substitute higher-priced products without an additional charge, and generally bend the rules.
- Threaten to never do business with the company again. Sometimes this is just a veiled threat, and sometimes it's sincere. Regardless, even if it's just bluster, it's bluster that a customer can easily share with anyone and everyone who will listen, thanks to the digital soapbox that social media gives us.

Excerpted from: *The Effortless Experience: Conquering the New Battleground for Customer Loyalty* by Matthew Dixon, Nick Toman, and Rick Delisi.

Power Points Worth Repeating

- Educate your associates that saying no frequently destroys any customer goodwill previously generated.

- Creating solutions instead of saying no takes time and effort, but it's worth it.

- Always tell customers what you can do, not what you can't do.

- It's especially critical to preserve the customer relationship when customers are disappointed.

- Listening and acknowledging a customer's unhappiness are the first step to demonstrate that you hear him or her.

- Rules should be guidelines, not rigid policies that cannot be adjusted.

- If associates have little or no authority, it reflects poorly on the organization and does nothing to create long-lasting customer relationships.

- Apologies have been proven to make people more loyal than before, but only if handled correctly.

- Acknowledging past loyalty communicates appreciation and will pave the way toward restoring the relationship—especially when it comes to an angry customer.

6

Invite Me to Return

The food at City Crab and Seafood Company in Manhattan is delicious, but the cuisine is not the first thing I think of when I tell people about the restaurant. Instead I talk about a waiter; his name is Iron.

From the first day I walked into City Crab, Iron has been amazing. He was welcoming and engaging when he brought us our menus. He knew about every dish the restaurant served, and his service throughout the meal was wonderful. Then, when we were getting ready to leave, Iron told us how much he enjoyed serving us and expressed the hope that he would see us again soon. He handed me a card with his cell number and told us which days and shifts he usually worked. He suggested I text or call him directly whenever I wanted to have dinner at the restaurant. Essentially, he offered to be my personal waiter.

Competition for diners' dollars is fierce in New York. There are more than 10,000 restaurants in Manhattan. There are 700 just in our zip code. Although we have a few favorite places, we see Iron at City Crab more often than any other place. That's because each time we go, we know we are especially welcome. We feel as though we are with family. How can those other 10,000 restaurants compete with that?

"Where's my invitation?"

In my first book, *The Welcomer Edge*, I explained how each successful customer encounter involves three essential elements: the greet, the assist, and the leave-behind. Most people understand the importance of the first two. If you're in customer service, you know the customer should be greeted first and then offered help. It's the leave-behind—the words and actions that express the interest in the customer's return—that seems the hardest of the three to remember and act on. And yet, repeat business with loyal customers is the central motivating goal of just about every business.

The leave-behind represents any number of little things that associates can do and say to make customers want to visit again. Just as with Iron, our waiter at City Crab, the leave-behind can be as simple as a card with your name and number or letting customers know your normal working hours. You can also offer to notify them about the arrival of new products they might like.

The point of every leave-behind is to make it easy for the customer to stay in touch. Every aspect of the business must reflect your expressed desire that he or she return and shop with you again. Even when you haven't made a sale, the human connection established while attempting to help the customer and the leave-behind can mark the start of a relationship that will result in future sales.

If you meet someone for the first time and have a great conversation at lunch, dinner, or coffee, the ultimate compliment is paid when one person says to the other, "Let's do this again. And let's do it soon." I think everyone who has ever been out on a first date understands the importance of "It would be so nice to see you again" and "How about next weekend?" Customers have the same need, the same expectation, whether they are aware of it or not. When you are invited to return, it makes you feel wanted and accepted. Those businesses that understand the value of inviting customers to return will reap the reward of happy and returning customers.

It doesn't matter whether you own a gas station, manage a customer service department, or a run a medical office—having a person from your staff communicating a message that you are eager to see the customer again can work wonders. It makes a customer feel good not only for the moment but also over and over again. The reason is found in the way our brains are hardwired. We all have what are called "mirror neurons" that prompt us to respond in a positive way to a positive, friendly request. Sincerely asking someone to visit again soon will automatically give a nudge toward doing so.

You might say to yourself, Do I really care whether I see the same person at the grocery store, mall, or restaurant? I know that most customers go back to the same coffee shop because the people behind the counter know their name, give them that welcoming smile, and say, "I will see you tomorrow." In any enterprise, knowing that someone wants to see you again makes you feel good. Any company with employees who are able to create and nurture a relationship and invite the customer to return has the formula for generating repeat business. As Steve Jobs said, "Sometimes people don't really know what they want until they get it."

Inviting customers to return works best in person-to-person encounters (opposed to e-mail blasts or mass text messaging). Every customer should know that a particular associate or representative thoroughly enjoyed helping him or her. Even with sales inquiries and other exchanges that are not face-to-face, it's critical to leave the customer with the impression that your inquiry by phone or e-mail was not a bother or an interruption. For those who are managing a large customer service department, assigning individual agents or small teams of representatives to handle a specific group of customers will provide the opportunity for this kind of personalized service.

A friend of ours who owns a spa mentioned that she, as well as her staff, communicates with every client that she wants them to return. She says, "Please come back." I suggested instead "I want to see you again." Her eyes lit up. She immediately grasped the impact a few words can make. "I" has the least number of letters, but the greatest quality of content. "I" means responsibility, sincerity, interest, and ownership.

I can't emphasize enough that feelings of loyalty naturally develop toward a person and not the business. City Crab is a great place, but I'm not so sure how often I would dine there if not for Iron. Be mindful of the importance of keeping employees who know how to welcome customers, who are experts in your products and services, and who are skilled in building customer relationships.

Checkout counter or Welcome Station?

Wal-Mart has been struggling, and the company has responded in part by experimenting with ways to make the checkout experience proceed more smoothly. The company experimented with a system where items could be purchased with a swipe of the phone at a kiosk, eliminating the cashier line altogether. The idea was to help shoppers avoid long lines, but the process turned out to be too complicated and confusing, and it was abandoned.

"Scan and Go" was a reaction to the disappointment with Wal-Mart's existing self-service checkout stations. These stations were designed to allow customers to check themselves out quickly, but, in fact, self-checkout lines are often slowed by customers who can't figure out what to do or by malfunctions in the equipment. Now Wal-Mart has decided to go in the other direction. It is testing the practice of staffing the self-checkout station, in order to add a personal touch and customer service to the experience. A similar concept called HybridCheckout allows the self-service customer to scan his or her items along with an attendant, eliminating the chance of customer frustration and combining the objectives of efficiency and personal service.[52]

These new ideas attest to the fact that while the checkout counter marks the end of each retail transaction, it should also mark the beginning of a customer loyalty journey. Customers crave human interaction that leaves them with the feeling that they'd like to return. They enjoy the control of scanning their own items but also want to speak to Jane at the checkout counter, if only for a moment. In that sense, every checkout counter should be considered a "Welcome Station." When the attendant or cashier at a Welcome Station is patient and caring and offers the opportunity for customers to ask questions, customers remember and want to buy there again.

Here are some suggestions for transforming a checkout counter into a Welcome Station:

- Staff the counter with frontline associates who can personalize the encounter. Just noticing what the customer has purchased or what a person is wearing is an important first step. I appreciate when a representative says to me "I like that yogurt flavor, too," or "That's a great tie you are wearing." As long as the feeling is genuine, it will make a human connection.

- Instruct cashiers to introduce themselves even if their name is on their badge: "Hi! I'm Mary. I'm happy to help you."

- Make sure cashiers understand the importance of thanking customers for their purchases and using their name. Many times customers pay with a credit card. The associate knows their name. Saying "Thank you, Mr. Smith, and have a great rest of the day" can make a customer feel special. Remember that "Customer Rage Study" in chapter 5. Eighty percent of survey respondents said they want to be thanked for their business, but only about one-third said they actually ever heard a thank-you. This simple gesture can help your company stand out from the crowd.

- Have your receipts do the inviting too. Companies can include a QR code on the receipt that signs people up for newsletters, special offers, or some type of promotion if they shop again. By including this, you are inviting your customers to return again.

Communicating to customers that you were so happy to help them today (and that you would love to help them in the future) leaves them with a good impression. Yes, you really do want them to return. And they will. These added steps may increase the length of each transaction by a few seconds, but you will find it is time well spent.

Please call us back

Voicemail remains an important resource in a world of text, e-mail, and chat. The human voice is more personal, more expressive, and more likely to make an emotional connection. If you have to set up a delivery date, confirm a reservation, or promote a new service, leaving a voice message is another opportunity to show customers that they are important and valued and their business appreciated.

Here is a sample script that can turn a simple voicemail message into a critical component of the customer journey:

1. *"Hi, Mr. Smith. My name is William."* Speak slowly and distinctly. Always use the name of the person you are calling and your own name.

2. *"I hope your day is going well."* Add something nice and welcoming. A warm wish that the customer's day is going well makes an instant emotional connection.

3. *"I'm happy to let you know that your furniture has arrived in our warehouse and we're ready to schedule a convenient delivery date."* The message is clear, concise, and informative.

4. *"Please call me at 800-555-9876. Once again, that's 800-555-9876. Ask for William."* It's important to repeat the number.

5. *"If I'm not available, you can also speak to Tim or Mary. They have your file. They can help you, too."* Additional information gives the customer a sense of choice.

6. *"Our hours are Monday through Friday, 8 a.m. to 5 p.m., and Saturdays from 10 a.m. to 6 p.m."* By providing hours of operation, you spare the customer the need to look up the information before returning the call.

7. *"Mr. Smith, we appreciate your business. We look forward to hearing from you at your earliest convenience."* Thanking the customer in the message is thoughtful and appreciated.

It may not always be possible to invite the customer to call back a specific person in a call center environment, but with the proper training, technology, and processes in place, representatives can still say, "I really enjoyed speaking with you today or handling your e-mail request and would like to personally serve you again. If I am not available, I work in a small team, and any one of our team members would be happy to help. That's what we are here for."

Human resource departments should look at hiring college-educated associates who see positions in customer service as a profession and not just a stepping-stone to another job. Representatives who excel at knowing the product, personalizing the interaction, and making all customers feel welcomed and important and that their business is appreciated should be paid a wage equal to those in the fields of account management and marketing.

When properly run, contact centers can be very effective to help maintain relationships with loyal customers. Unfortunately, senior executives seldom appreciate the potential value offered by call centers in this regard. More often than not, contact centers are viewed as "cost centers"—drains on the company's coffers instead of tools for customer retention. In order to earn an ROI from contact centers, companies must have strategic plans that include investment in technology to help representatives provide customers with a seamless service experience.

From our research and experience, many contact center managers miss the opportunity to support their own cause. The ROI for their departments is rarely computed to determine how service and support affect future purchase behaviors of customers. This information, coupled with the action of your customer base, can provide your department with important data to reinforce budget negotiations and requests for added staff, training, and technology.

Every department in an organization has value. Managers of contact centers must document and demonstrate their worth by gathering data. But how the data are collected can make a big difference. For instance, if a call center attempts to collect satisfaction and loyalty information immediately following each contact, the responses may be faulty. A significant component of a department's loyalty value is based on word-of-mouth behavior following the call. Customers who interact with your company's contact center need some time to reflect on their experience and then tell others about it.

Assessing a representative sample of customers who communicate with your contact center five to 10 days after the interaction will garner much clearer data on the effect the call center is having on purchasing behavior. This is especially true when the customer is expecting a promised fulfillment or awaiting the resolution of an issue that will occur sometime after the contact.

Here are the four primary ROI outcomes following any contact center exchange:

1. **Enhanced Positive ROI**—The call had the effect of increasing already-existing customer loyalty. In this scenario, the customer might purchase more of a particular product because he or she learned something new during the interaction or because the representative with whom he or she communicated built a stronger relationship that resulted in the customer purchasing more from your company than from your competitors.

2. **Restored Positive ROI**—This pertains to the "saved" customer. The interaction persuades the customer to stay despite a negative experience. Perhaps the customer purchased a product that did not last as long as expected and he or she was thinking of not

purchasing that particular product ever again. But, because the call rectified the issue quickly and satisfactorily, the customer remained loyal. Experienced and customer-friendly agents are able to save millions of dollars every year by converting a dissatisfied consumer into a brand advocate.

3. **Negative ROI**—The call is handled poorly, and the customer later expresses the intent to purchase from a competitor. Customers stop purchasing the brand altogether if they feel they are not treated appropriately by the company representative or do not like the company's policies.

4. **Zero ROI**—Interactions may not affect the purchasing behavior of the customer at all. Sometimes, the customer loves a particular brand so much that no matter how the interaction is handled, he or she will continue to purchase.

While the dollar value of word of mouth can't always be accurately assessed, such random surveys can help you discover what percentage of your customers told others about their experiences with your company. You can also identify the type of people they told (neighbors, friends, business associates, etc.) and how (traditional word of mouth or social media sites).

The contact center can be the heart and home of your company because call center representatives speak to more customers than any other department. The rep talks to customers an average of 100 times a day, or 20,000 people a year. It makes sense to invest in such a valuable resource. Companies with well-managed call centers that hire the right people, compensate them appropriately, and reward and acknowledge superior performers will never have to worry about a new competitor picking away at their customer base one customer at a time.

Managing the customer relationship

Our friend Bonnie complained to us that her company recently installed an automated customer relations management system. To her disappointment, the new CRM system now automates the leave-behind, removing Bonnie's personal touch and almost instantly putting up a wall of anonymity between Bonnie and her customers.

Bonnie has always been very good at personally inviting her customers to return. She sells a line of fashion accessories through a marketing approach similar to the Tupperware party concept. Prospective buyers come to her home or other locations because she sent them an invitation in the mail or by e-mail or making the old-fashioned phone call. Her prospects are people she knows well or friends of friends who recommend her line. She rarely has the need to advertise, and people are always attracted in large numbers to her events.

One of the many ways Bonnie nurtures her clientele is by sending a personalized e-mail to each person who attended a "party." These e-mails not only detail what was purchased but also reflect Bonnie's actual conversations with each person. She includes wishes such as "Have a great time on the trip" and "Good luck with that college application." These follow-up e-mails let her customers know they are more than just receipts to Bonnie.

The new CRM system, by contrast, is cold and efficient. It allows Bonnie and other reps to have a clear and accurate record of their customers and purchasing histories. It's a great labor saver. After an event, it generates an *automated e-mail* thanking the people for attending and itemizing all of the items that were purchased, and it is signed with Bonnie's name. But the system prevents Bonnie from having any personalized communications with her customers. She quickly realized that the CRM system wasn't devoted to cultivating "customer relationships" at all. It was designed to allow management to keep track of her contacts and their purchases.

This is another example where technology creates efficiency but has built-in limitations that end up damaging the human connection. Relationships are cultivated on a person-to-person basis, not through impersonal automated "thank-you" e-mails. Bonnie's employer has allowed technology to eliminate her critical human touch and replace true customer relationships with robotic account management.

Bonnie is one of the most successful sales associates in the history of her company. She achieved this level of excellence and stature by treating her customer as a person first and customer second. Now she fears her long list of customers and prospects will slowly shrink over time because what was once "up close and personal" has become another run-of-the mill automated communication process that makes doing business with Bonnie not particularly that special.

Inviting the customer to return is one of most important steps in continuing the customer journey. Those words have meaning only if they are said one person to another, solidifying the human connection.

Power Points Worth Repeating

- The point of every leave-behind is to make it easy for the customer to stay in touch.

- Even when you haven't made a sale, the human connection established while attempting to help the customer can result in future sales.

- When a customer is invited to return, it makes the customer feel wanted and accepted.

- Sincerely asking a customer to visit again soon will automatically give him or her a nudge toward doing so.

- In any enterprise, knowing that someone wants to see you again makes a person feel good.

- Creating small customer service teams within large call center environments helps to convey a feeling of personalized service.

- "I" has the least number of letters but the greatest quality of content, creating a personalized invitation to return.

- The check-out counter should mark the beginning of the customer journey, not the end.

- Consider paying frontline associates who excel at knowing the product, personalizing the encounter, and making customers feel welcomed and important wages equal to those of account management and marketing.

- Relationships are cultivated on a person-to-person basis, not through impersonal automated "thank-you" e-mails.

7

Show Me I Matter

Remember Joe Girard, the world's greatest car salesperson? Joe saw the lifetime value of every customer and acted accordingly. He won loyal customers in part by providing them with exceptional service for years following each sale.

But how could a salesperson like Girard make sure his customers received such good care for their cars? He did it by befriending the members of the service department at his dealership. He told them he loved them, took them to dinner, made sure they knew how important they were to him. The service department members, in turn, gave Joe's customers the red carpet treatment when they came in for maintenance and repairs. Service technicians met Joe's customers at the curb and frequently didn't bother charging them for small parts and minor tasks. Every time Joe's customers brought their cars in for maintenance, they were reminded how important they were.[53] They responded with the kind of customer loyalty that landed him in the *Guinness Book* as the world's greatest car salesperson.

Every customer enjoys feeling important, and the continued engagement and loyalty of such customers is vital to every company's success. *So why do so many companies fail to make their customers feel important and special?*

Falling through the cracks

Following the leave-behind, the next most important step in the customer relationship is reaching out to express your appreciation for that customer's business. This crucial step provides a unique opportunity for a true human connection, specifically because it happens *after* the sale. In order to develop authentic customer loyalty, you must make sure that the shopping experience feels like more than merely a transactional exchange. The reason, like so many other concepts in this book, is rooted in our humanity. We are all innately suspicious of someone who seems to lose interest in us *after* money has changed hands. People just hate feeling seduced and abandoned. People like feeling important and special.

Companies rarely reach out to customers with a meaningful and personalized dialogue about the product and its use. Perhaps a perfunctory thank-you is sent by e-mail. For most businesses, after-sale follow-up tends to fall through the cracks in the course of getting daily business done.

If managers are oblivious to this problem, it's because very few executives test their own systems by buying something from their company and experiencing the entire purchasing process from a customer's point of view. I suspect that many managers must undergo the feeling of being abandoned after money has changed hands before they'll be motivated to make changes.

The tremendous success of the car service Uber is due in large part to how well the company uses technology to provide a high level of customer care, even after the ride. The first time I used Uber, things did not go particularly smoothly. However, the way Uber resolved my problems left me more impressed with the company than if my first ride had gone without a hitch.

We scheduled our Uber ride on a Saturday morning, and the car arrived within five minutes, right on schedule. I really like how the Uber app provides customers with a timed countdown to the driver's arrival. However, not long after we were on our way, I received a text message from an Uber driver, letting us know he was waiting in front of our building. Whoops! Apparently, another resident had requested Uber at the same time we did. I told our driver about our mistake, and he assured us that we should just cancel the other reservation, and it would all work out.

The next day, I received this e-mail from Uber.

Dear Richard,

Did you mean to contact Uber Support?

Please reply to this email if there were any issues we need to look into. I'll be happy to help.

Happy Ubering!

All the best,

Les

Uber Support

I realized I must have hit "support" on the Uber app when I was trying to reach the other driver to cancel our original reservation. Uber received my accidental message, which had no content, but instead of ignoring it, the company did everything right. It:

- Sent me a personalized e-mail using my first name

- Asked whether I still needed assistance

- Offered to help and assured me I wasn't a bother

- Wished me a good day—Happy Ubering!

- Personalized the e-mail with a signature from Les

Uber was proactive. Uber treated me like a person. And Uber did not send a response with that line we all see too often: "DO NOT REPLY."

I e-mailed Les and explained what happened. He replied almost immediately, and his response made me feel that Uber valued me and my patronage:

Hi Richard,

Thanks for writing back and letting me know. Happy to help.

So sorry to hear about the trouble here! I've gone ahead and refunded $8 back to your method of payment and requested an updated receipt be emailed to you. You should see the change reflected in your account within 1–3 business days.

Thanks for letting us know and please let me know if I can help with anything else. Happy Ubering!

All the best,

Les

I was very impressed with Uber's system for resolving issues; the company managed to do many simple things fast and well. Uber's example serves as a vivid reminder that most after-sale experiences are not like this at all. I'm particularly surprised how brick-and-mortar stores today offer excellent service prior to the sale but then very little after-sale continuity involving goods that require delivery and installation. Especially for local businesses that rely on word-of-mouth endorsements, delivery is an integral part of the customer experience. How does it make sense to take a customer's money and then turn over the rest of the purchase experience to another department or a third-party vendor?

Another personal experience: my wife and I purchased a wall unit, and the interaction in the store with the salesperson was perfect. He was knowledgeable, attentive, and thorough. He came to our apartment to measure the space to make sure the furniture would fit. He listened to our concerns and responded. The whole process was a flawless customer experience.

Shortly before Christmas, we were informed that the wall unit we purchased in October had arrived and was ready for delivery. We were given contact information for Anne, the customer service representative in the delivery department, so we could arrange a convenient delivery date. When our first call wasn't returned after three hours, we called again and learned that Anne had no record of our order. Even after we'd given her our name and order number, she had difficulty locating our wall unit.

Anne first told us the unit would be installed on December 28. We were pleased because we were having guests on New Year's Day. Two hours later she called back to say our furniture required a different team of delivery personnel, and that team would not be available until after the New Year. She would have to reschedule and promised to call back. We were disappointed, but what could we do?

We waited a week for Anne to call us back, and then we contacted our salesperson to let him know that we seemed to have fallen into delivery limbo. Two days later, we left another message for Anne. Four hours later, we called again, and this time Anne behaved as though she did not know who we were. Then we learned for the first time that the unit delivery would require two visits: one from a moving team and another from an assembly team. Eventually the teams were scheduled, the rest of the process went smoothly, and we love the piece. But we will never forget how hard we had to work just to get something we'd paid for months ago. We were left with a bad taste and now are reluctant to shop at that store again. Obviously, delivery is part of the experience and a way to show customers they matter.

Take a good look at any company that is known for being "loved" by legions of loyal customers. You will discover that the company has instituted any number of consistent procedures and practices that assure customers of their importance—little things that most companies neglect to include in their overall customer experience strategies. It's time to take a look at this aspect of your offerings to your customers. If your follow-up communications are careless and somehow suggest that you take your customers for granted, those customers will never love your company, will never give you their loyalty, and will not remain customers for the long term.

Put it in writing

I remember when I first arrived at sleep-away camp how excited I was to receive a letter from my parents or grandparents. The notes were warm, loving, and upbeat and filled with exciting news from back home. When I was reading them, I could picture my parents or grandparents saying the words. It was almost like they were standing next to me, even though they were more than a hundred miles away.

For centuries, the written word was the sole mode of long-distance communication, and written words have always been effective at conveying all kinds of feelings: passion, sincerity, love, and even anger and disappointment. Writing remains important today, through e-mail and text messaging, but I get frustrated at times how impersonal these written communications have grown. One of the best and easiest ways to show people they matter is through communication. There's really no reason why e-mails and text need to read as though they were composed by robots. Even adding the word "Hi" can warm up the message and make it sound friendlier and more appealing. Remember the Uber communication above.

The same can be said for all those formal e-mails we receive after making an online purchase. Some of these e-mails don't even address you by name, as if they are saying, "Hey, you!" Most e-mails go immediately into a scripted text without ever expressing the wish that the recipient is having a good day.

An e-mail can be as personalized and warm as a letter or even a phone call. Here are a few do's and don'ts for communicating with customers online in a way that reminds them they matter to you.

Do . . .

- Open with a greeting that states "We hope you're having a good day."

- Send them a personal e-mail when they register for an account; make them feel welcome and that their business will be appreciated. There is only one opportunity to make a good first impression.

- Give them various delivery options; it helps the customer feel more in control.

- Keep them posted on the status of orders, especially customized products. A biweekly contact keeps the customer updated.

- Offer them an easy way to get help, like an online chat with a person instead of the standard FAQs.

- Thank them for their business and communicate that you want to hear from them if they are not totally satisfied.

Don't . . .

- Force them to enter their e-mail address before viewing your site. They would never give their cell phone number to a stranger because he or she might someday become a friend, so why should they share their e-mail before they even know what your site offers?

- Send them e-mails every day after their first purchase. If you really want to keep in touch, allow them to select their communication preferences first.

- Create e-mails with the subject line "Do not reply to this e-mail." It frustrates customers, especially when the message notifies customers that their service is being renewed automatically.

- Give them a delivery date and then follow up with an e-mail stating that the item is out of stock. A customer wants to know immediately whether the item is available and can then choose to order or not. Make sure your system is up to date and has the correct information and inventory.

The best after-sale communications are the ones that express gratitude and appreciation for the customer's patronage. Most e-commerce sites skip this step and send unwanted e-mail solicitations instead. If I order paper plates from Party City, suddenly I'm getting daily promotional e-mails announcing their specials for the day. Maybe Party City makes more sales this way, but what Party City can't count is the number of customers turned off by this approach. Sending daily deal e-mails is is not how you show customers that they matter. Instead, it gives customers a good reason to unsubscribe and shop elsewhere.

The marketers at Jacob's Pillow Dance Theater in Massachusetts are careful not to send out e-mails to patrons without adding something of value as a part of the communication. About a week after my wife and I attended a performance, we were delighted to receive an e-mail with a link to video interviews with the dance troupe's members. We had already enjoyed watching the dancers and connecting with them from an artistic perspective, and then we were offered the opportunity to hear their voices and learn their life stories. It was interesting and meaningful and, above all, communicated to us that Jacob's Pillow patrons matter to the institution.

Just listen

One of the best ways to remind customers that they matter is to demonstrate you're interested in what they have to say. "Survey" is sometimes thought of as a nasty word. However, customer feedback is essential to improving service if acquired in the right way and then implemented to make positive changes. At our company, TCFCR, we have found that customers are more than happy to complete customer surveys, even in a 10- or 15-minute telephone interview, if:

- The surveys are conducted at the convenience of the customer.

- The interviewer is pleasant and professional.

- Customers feel that the company is going to use the feedback to make changes that are beneficial for them.

A lot of companies have an automated follow-up survey immediately after the customer has called for support. The pitfall of that system is that problems prompting many support calls are not resolved right away. Asking customers whether they're satisfied when they've just gotten off the phone with the company makes it difficult to obtain an accurate gauge of brand loyalty and service satisfaction.

When I called Verizon after losing my cell phone, the Verizon representative listened patiently and then told me that I needed to call Asurion, Verizon's insurance provider, in order to arrange for a replacement phone. I thanked her and hung up—but wondered why the Verizon representative couldn't just transfer my call and spare me the need to repeat my story.

Then, before I could punch in the number for Asurion, an automated call from Verizon requested I participate in a survey about my recent experience with its customer service representative. Now, what was the point? How could I possibly rate the customer experience when my problem, at that moment, remained unresolved? The follow-up call was a total waste of my time and Verizon's resources.

When you are able to tell customers that their opinions matter following the sale, you help confirm their decision to do business with you. Most organizations recognize the importance and value of having processes in place to react to issues but don't have procedures or policies or don't train their staffs to show customers they still count just as a course of doing business. In most cases, it is no more complex than logging a simple follow-up phone call or text.

For instance, a mother of the bride purchases a beautiful dress for her daughter's once-in-a-lifetime event. The boutique does all the right things. Knowledgeable sales professionals, excellent fitters, and tailors all do their jobs well and on time. But I would say the job is not done until the week after the wedding, when a salesperson picks up the phone to ask about the event and how the dress looked. Was the party everything she envisioned? Did the customer receive any compliments? How did she feel in the dress? Those questions would make the customer feel appreciated and glad she bought that special dress at the boutique. Even if this is the last evening dress that the customer ever needs to buy, she will recommend the store to all her friends.

A great way to tell customers they matter is to ask your most loyal customers whether they would post a review on your company web page or on social media. Social media can be tricky, however. Yelp, for instance, has a system for filtering out glowing reviews if they read too much like the customer is either doing the business owner a personal favor or receiving some kind of an inducement for posting a positive review. If your customer's review isn't posted, the customer might feel that you're responsible for wasting his or her time and effort—the very last thing you'd want to do.

Caring shouldn't be an accident

Companies have processes and policies in place that focus on how individual interactions should be handled. However, demonstrating genuine concern and care after the conclusion of the interaction is something that many companies do not consider. When it does happen, it's just an accident. A plan for this segment of the customer experience, what happens after the sale, must be part of a new paradigm. Without it, accidents will happen and customers will be lost.

Most companies have CRMs, customer relations management systems, that track customer purchases, but these systems are rarely used to full advantage. The data provide a wealth of information that can be used to show customers you care. Remember the pillows we bought from Macy's about three years ago? We decided we wanted to buy a few more. Easy. We called Rochelle, our salesperson (see chapter 4).

Not only did she have all our information regarding shipping but also she had a record of the specific styles and colors we had purchased. She had immediate access to the inventory and current prices. Rochelle told us that our particular pillow was being discontinued but there were four left in stock that could be shipped the following day. We decided we wanted all four because we liked the pillows so much. Macy's doubled the sale, and we were happy. The automated system gave us personal care.

Some businesses, though, don't see the value of keeping information, which baffles me. My wife bought an evening gown from a small store and left it there for alterations for several weeks while we were on vacation. When she returned to pick it up, her salesperson greeted her with, "I'm glad you came today. I was just ready to delete your name from my records." My wife likes the store, but the comment was an automatic turnoff. She was being removed from the database. Obviously the store had no interest in her continued patronage.

I know whenever a sales associate tells me that my prior purchase history and account information are no longer available, I always feel as though the store considers me irrelevant. The message is that I am not "customer worthy"—a mild indignity compounded when I have to repeat or reenter information that the company should already have.

Recently a friend shared that she has no desire to be contacted by a company after the sale is complete. I can understand her feelings. If there was no connection or attempt to create a relationship during the transaction and sale, then reaching out afterward doesn't make sense. Everything about the customer experience has to be genuine or it loses its punch. If the salesperson didn't care in the first place, then of course my friend would perceive communication after the sale only as a bother. The new paradigm, the key to customer retention and loyalty, is the customer experience journey. A journey is, by definition, steps along a path that gets a person, the customer, from one place to another. The point is that the journey continues and never has to end.

From the research done by TCFCR, we have found that consumers are very pleased with how the interactions with company consumer affairs departments are handled. For the most part, the interaction between the company representative and the customer is considered to be "one and done," and customers have no expectation of being contacted afterward. Nonetheless, a good way to show customers they matter would be to send a personalized e-mail or letter referencing the original problem and letting them know the company appreciates their continued business.

In the e-commerce world, many companies send daily e-mails regarding sales and promotions. I think this is overkill because it communicates to the customer that the company cares more about pushing sales than it does about keeping in touch. As previously discussed, sending a personalized communication at an appropriate milestone demonstrates a more genuine interest in the customer relationship.

Most high-end retailers, with Nordstrom as a good example, encourage their sales personnel to keep in touch with customers. They send handwritten notes that thank them for their purchases and advise them of new merchandise and upcoming sales. The information you have about your customers is golden. How you handle that information reflects on your company's culture. Do you use your data to build loyalty with your customers, or does data interest you only in terms of efficiency and the short-term bottom line?

Power Points Worth Repeating

- Following the leave-behind, the next most important step is reaching out to customers afterward to express your appreciation for their business.

- To ensure customer loyalty, provide a shopping experience that feels like more than a mere transactional exchange.

- Brick-and-mortar stores fail to think of after-sales activities such as the delivery and installation process as part of the customer experience.

- There is no reason why an e-mail can't be as personalized and warm as a letter or even a phone call.

- The best after-sale communications are the ones that express gratitude and appreciation for the customer's patronage.

- Sending daily e-mail promotions gives the customers a good reason to unsubscribe and shop elsewhere in the future.

- One of the best ways to remind customers they matter is to demonstrate that you are interested in what they have to say.

- When you are able to tell customers their opinions matter after the sale, you help confirm their decision to do business with you.

- Most organizations recognize the importance of having procedures in place to react to issues but not to show customers their business counts.

- Asking customers to post reviews is a good way to show them they matter.

8

Surprise Me in Good Ways

Years ago, while on business in San Francisco, one of our clients specially arranged for me to stay at a small boutique hotel near Union Square. I do a great deal of traveling but still vividly remember the experience of driving up to the hotel for the first time and having the valet open the door of the taxi and take my bags out of the trunk with the warm greeting: "Mr. Shapiro, welcome to the Pan Pacific Hotel." That had never happened to me before, and its never happened since.

How did the hotel associate know my name? My guess is that he read my luggage tags while removing my bags from the cab. It was such a small gesture I couldn't believe how it affected me. I felt welcomed and appreciated before I'd even set foot inside. Then as soon as I approached the front desk in the third-floor lobby, one of the attendants behind the counter gave me a big smile and said, "Mr. Shapiro, we are so glad to see you today."

Needless to say, a few months later when I traveled again to San Francisco, I made sure I booked the Pan Pacific Hotel. I entered my room to discover that I had been complementary upgraded to a small suite. There was a large fruit basket on the table with a handwritten note: "Mr. Shapiro, we welcome you back to the Pan Pacific Hotel. We appreciate your business." I thought to myself, "Wow, they had selected my room before I even arrived."

All these small touches and courtesies showed a level of forethought and attention to detail I truly appreciated. I felt the hotel's management valued my business and, equally as important, wanted to see me again in the future. It's the little things that do make a difference. All it took was welcoming me by name and offering a sincere smile and a thoughtful handwritten note. Are any of these too much to ask? I think not. After all, almost 20 years later I still remember driving up to the hotel as if it were yesterday.

Decoding delight

Customer satisfaction is a minimal standard; loyal customer relationships are built around surprise and delight. Customers crave human interactions that leave them with the experience of feeling special, and nothing conveys specialness better than surprise.

By one estimate, adding some degree of surprise to any experience intensifies that experience by 400 percent.[54] When something nice is delivered as a surprise, it's four times as memorable and exciting as the same thing minus the surprise. Consider that whatever you can do for your customers, you can make four times as much impact by adding the element of surprise.

Surprise and delight rank high among the most effective marketing tools because they play into some very basic truths about human nature. Studies by neuroscientists suggest that human brains are "designed to crave the unexpected."[55] Surprises introduce us to new stimuli, and new stimuli encourage learning—which can result in customers being more receptive to buying new products, upgrading services, and more.[56] Advertising strategist Scott Redick writes, "When developing an advertising campaign we are often too focused on the question of 'What do we need to say?' Instead, we should focus on the question of 'What expectations do our customers and prospects hold, and how can we turn those on their head?'"[57]

Another study published in the *Harvard Business Review* notes that cruise lines apply many operating principles for creating customer surprise and delight using the following three basic principles for creating memorable experiences:

- Segment the pleasure—Pack lots of experiences into a short vacation.

- Create rituals—Midnight buffets and captain's dinners are special.

- Finish strong—End each day on a high note, with raffles and contests. End the cruise with the captain's dinner and pass out keepsakes upon reaching home-port.[58]

As a practical matter, it could be that only your best customers are deserving of special treatment and surprises. Many businesses receive about 80 percent of their revenues from 20 percent of their customers, in accord with the so-called Pareto principle. With that in mind, it's smart to look at ways to segment your customer base so that those customers who spend a lot and have the potential to spend more are singled out for special treatment—because they obviously consider your business to be special.

Zingerman's foods of Ann Arbor, Michigan, had this way of surprising a customer who had made a large order with the company during the holiday season. Sometime in the following September, the customer received a box with a cake and the following note: "When you needed a gift last holiday season, you chose Zingerman's. That means a lot to us. We're gearing up for this year's rush, and we'd like to help you make this season a delicious one, too. Thank you and Happy Holidays! The Whole Gang at Zingerman's Mail Order."

Sometimes you might consider going out of your way to provide a surprise for a top customer you've disappointed. A few years ago, a good friend of mine, Mike, was invited to dinner on a Friday evening by some friends, a married couple, who had always told him about the short ribs served at their favorite restaurant in northern New Jersey. After they were seated, however, they learned that short ribs were a special dish served only on Saturdays. When Mike's friends asked the manager whether perhaps a special order could be prepared, the manager apologized, explaining that the ribs took many hours of cooking time.

The next day, Saturday, the restaurant manager appeared at the couples' front door with an entire meal: short ribs, a salad, and a tasty dessert. The couple was shocked but thrilled. The restaurant's manager demonstrated that their business was truly appreciated, and the couple's loyalty to the restaurant is rock solid.

Ideas are all around you

When clients visit our offices for the first time, many of them are in for a special surprise. We have an extensive collection of vintage advertising memorabilia representing our clients' firms. These posters, signs, and knickknacks are all very unusual and interesting to look at, but our clients are naturally most attracted to the ones that represent their own companies. Some of our client companies have been in business for nearly a century, and the product advertisements from the last 100 years are fascinating.

I have been collecting this memorabilia for about 20 years, and I never tire of finding new items in antique shops and fairs and online auction sites. I'm very pleased with what the décor says about how we feel about our clients. It not only makes them feel comfortable and welcomed in an unusual way but also communicates that our staff is mindful of their company histories and values and that they have created brands lasting through many generations of customers.

Displaying your company's history helps to create a special kind of connection—a connection that can help create an instant bond between your clients and your staff.

If you apply this thought to everything you do, there's no end to small, inexpensive changes you can make in order to enhance your customers' experience. You might be thinking that you don't have a budget line for surprises, but surprises don't always involve a significant outlay of cash. For instance, at the homepage of the consulting group Surprise Industries, they've collected examples of otherwise mundane web pages that manage to surprise and delight their users. A few special companies have designed the presentation of run-of-the-mill functions that everyone sees—such as the log-in page, the terms of service page, and the subscriber buttons—in ways that communicate how they care about your experience. The fact that it takes a little thought to make such ordinary pages different communicates to users that this is a thoughtful company.

There is an Italian restaurant in Cincinnati called Boca that touts its service standard as "BPA"—blow people away. That's what customers come to Boca expecting, and that's how employees understand their roles. A busboy overhearing a customer expressing disappointment about forgetting to order the Brussels sprouts might return to the table with a free sample of the dish—without ever being asked.

While visiting Boca for a business meeting, a Procter & Gamble executive was inspired by the BPA philosophy to initiate a series of random acts of kindness through social media and consumer support lines for Secret antiperspirant. When an American woman living in Spain wrote on Secret's Facebook fan page that she felt frustrated she could no longer get her favorite Secret scent overseas, P&G decided to send her the product free of charge. Then the Secret brand managers ran into a problem: customs regulations restricted the product from being shipped to Spain from the United States through the mail. That obstacle, however, merely helped sweeten the surprise. P&G arranged for a company executive to bring the package of Secret products with him on his vacation to Italy, and then he mailed it to the customer in Spain from within the European Union. Of course, the customer was delighted.

Now Secret's brand managers try to use BPA in response to complaints, as well. When a woman contacted P&G to complain about the lack of ethnic diversity among the models featured in Secret promotions, not only did P&G make changes to its promotions campaign but also the company used the BPA approach to go beyond thanking the woman for her constructive criticism. The woman, who coaches disadvantaged youths on their job-seeking skills, received a case of Secret to distribute to the young people.[59]

Here are some low-cost ways to surprise your customers and differentiate your company from the others:

- **Send handwritten thank-you notes**—Sales professionals at Nordstrom frequently do that. However, in addition to acknowledging the purchase immediately after the sale, I'm suggesting that you send a personal e-mail or note to customers periodically.

It could be six months after a large purchase or even on the anniversary of the transaction. Every business is different, but think of ways to thank customers after the sale has been finalized. My wife and I had our newspaper rerouted during a two-week summer vacation with our family. When I received the last paper the day we left, there was a yellow sticky note attached. "Thank you so much and I hope your family enjoys the rest of their summer, signed Sandra." That was totally unexpected, felt sincere, and put a smile on my face.

- **Educate your customers**—As in the example about Jacob's Pillow in chapter 7, where they included a link to a video interview of the dancers from the performance we attended. Consider sending an e-mail to your customers that teaches something they may not know or would not have access to.

- **Feature customers in newsletters**—Most people want to be recognized. If a customer has employed your service in a very unique manner, ask him or her to share the story with other customers. Blank Label, the online custom shirt site that I first wrote about in *The Welcomer Edge*, has an entire section on its website called "Customer Stories." Its heading is "thoughts from our customers, many of whom have made Blank Label their new standard."

- **Send good customers a free goodie or a surprise gift**—Recently, a friend told me about a company that sent a small package of chocolate mints along with an order that had been delayed beyond the original estimated delivery date. It made her feel special. She also received a phone call a week later to make sure that she received it and that it met her expectations.

Those actions not only demonstrate customer appreciation but also show customers they are unique.

- **Make a donation to a charity**—Offer to make a donation to a charity of the customer's choice. It could be a small amount honoring a good customer or one who just made a large purchase.

- **Invite customers to a meet and greet or special event**— My wife was invited to attend a book signing for a cookbook. She not only got to meet the author but also met some new friends.

- **Send a discount coupon or a free upgrade**—Sending an unexpected upgrade for a new technology product or an extra discount for your services is also a nice way to keep in touch. But you should try to time the reward with the transaction's anniversary date; it could be a month, three months, or a year. People appreciate the awards, but if they are tied into a specific reason or date, they will have more meaning.

- **Offer to join a loyalty club or fan page**—Many companies offer customers rewards for visiting their Facebook pages or sending out a retweet about a sale or other promotion. I definitely believe loyalty programs can work, but they should be personalized so that accumulating points is not the only reason for staying in the program.

- **Ask customers for their opinions**—This works well in almost any business, and not only will the customer be surprised that you want to know what he or she thinks but also your organization will be surprised with the number of great ideas.

Before you decide to deliver a surprise, however, you also must consider the risk. It could be that the surprise is unpleasant and unwanted. In other words, do your homework. Lands' End, the clothing retailer, once partnered with the publisher of *GQ* magazine and sent complimentary copies of the magazine to its male customers (female Lands' End customers had received copies of *Glamour* or *Vogue* in the past). Unfortunately, the magazine that month featured a scantily clad image of the model Emily Ratajkowski. Lands' End executives apologized profusely and announced that in the future they would send out issues of *Condé Nast Traveler*, which would have been the safer choice from the start.[60]

The thing to remember about surprises is that customers are not likely to articulate that they wish they had more of them in their daily shopping routine. The inherent benefit created by any surprise is that it comes from an unexpected place, so a lot of thought needs to be put into any such idea in advance. All surprises should have the goal of building stronger customer relationships. Any idea for a surprise that risks putting even a few customer relationships at risk is an idea that needs more work.

Pay it forward

The subject matter of these final three chapters can be summed up as acknowledgment, appreciation, and delight. Of the eight steps described in this book, the final three are perhaps the most difficult ones to implement because acknowledgment, appreciation, and delight have nothing to do with closing sales and raising short-term revenue. These stages of the customer journey, which come after the transaction is complete, are all about building human relationships for long-term customer loyalty. Although just about every business owner and executive will extol the benefits of customer loyalty, few of them are willing to make the investments necessary to nurture that loyalty through the steps and examples provided. Customer loyalty may be your company's goal, but you will not meet that goal until making human connections becomes a company priority.

The truth is that the human need for acknowledgment, appreciation, and delight can be fulfilled through all eight steps of the customer journey. The first five—welcoming, offering attention, being responsive, sharing knowledge, and giving your all—involve useful, practical ideas toward closing more sales. But in a truly customer-centric organization, each one of these early stages can and should be executed with acknowledgment, appreciation, and delight in mind, as well. Is that a tall order? Of course it is. But just like truth, justice, or any other lofty ideal, making the human connection is something worth reaching for even if it is not always attained. To borrow a phrase from my grandson's summer camp: take pride in the effort. Even if you try and fail to make a human connection, the effort is always worth making.

When I visit a lively, well-run coffee shop, I enjoy just standing back and watching the interactions between regular customers and the staff behind the counter. There are big smiles in every direction, the staff knows the regular customers' preferred orders, and, most importantly, both the servers and the customers know each other's names. The next time you visit such a shop on a busy morning, listen to the banter between customers and the staff and you will hear those three essential touchstones of human connection: acknowledgment, appreciation, and delight.

Javier, whom I met while he was working at a coffee shop in 2007, is a young man who knows in his heart that this human connection is what coffee shop customers are looking for, beyond their morning bagel and coffee. They want a familiar greeting, a warm smile, and a delightful experience. Javier was such a natural in making human connections and impressed me so much that I eventually hired him to work for our company.

Frequently, I ask exceptional frontline associates, such as Javier, exactly why they make such an effort to connect with their customers. What compels them to treat their customers so well in a job where polite indifference is the norm? What I usually find is that exceptional associates are in the habit of extending warm and welcoming feelings to just about every person they meet. One young man named Jefferson, working at a Starbucks on 14th Street in Manhattan, gave me this simple answer: it's more fun to be this way. In Jefferson's experience, everyone (including himself) has a better time when he treats each person—even someone he's just met—as though he's known that person forever.

Jefferson also told me that he believes in the concept of "paying it forward." As he sees it, if a customer who's having a bad day ends up with his or her spirits lifted thanks to Jefferson's warmth and kindness, then that customer in turn might pay the favor forward and help lift up someone else's spirits. In a kind of ripple effect, you can never know how the acknowledgment, appreciation, and delight you share with a customer today will touch the other people in that customer's life throughout the day.

I loved the 2000 movie *Pay It Forward*, in which a little boy's homework assignment—propose an idea to change the world—results in the practice of paying good deeds forward, so that the recipient of each good deed must do three good deeds for others. Every day, exceptional frontline associates like Jefferson embody the ethos of pay it forward. Jefferson assumes that his role involves much more than serving coffee, just the way my dad saw his role as much more than selling menswear. Jefferson wants to put a smile on the face of everyone who walks into his

Starbucks, trusting that some of those smiles will inspire more smiles on the faces of people Jefferson will never meet.

Pay it forward is really the ultimate expression of customer service, because it's a practice that puts people before profits. As my dad would say, it's about the customer's state of mind, not the customer's form of payment. A pay-it-forward culture at your company will naturally reap dividends in terms of customer loyalty and repeat patronage because customers will naturally keep returning to anyone capable of giving them this feeling. And they in turn will tell their friends about you—in person and through social media—as a way of paying it forward.

Pay it forward works because it makes your employees and your customers feel great about themselves and each other—and what goes around comes around. If we all practiced pay it forward, in everything we do, the world truly would be a better place.

Power Points Worth Repeating

- It's the little things that can make a customer feel welcome: using the person's name, a sincere smile, and a thoughtful handwritten note.

- With customer satisfaction as a minimal standard, loyal customer relationships are built around surprise and delight.

- Customers crave human interactions that leave them with the experience of feeling special, and nothing conveys specialness better than surprise.

- Look at ways to segment and reward those customers who are high volume and those who have the potential to spend more.

- Every business is unique; think of ways to thank customers after the sale has been finalized.

- Consider sending an e-mail to customers that teaches them something they may not know or would not have access to.

- Customer loyalty may be your company's goal, but you will not meet that goal until making human connections becomes a company priority.

- Even if you try and fail to make a human connection, the effort is always worth making.

- Pay it forward is the ultimate expression of customer service because it's a practice that puts people before profits.

Appendix I
Repeat Business Scorecard

It's an old adage that you should "inspect what you expect." Once your organization fully comprehends the concept that the customer journey starts with the first encounter and should never end, it's critical to evaluate how your organization is meeting each of the eight steps from the customers' perspective. TCFCR has provided two survey questions for each element. Once you are a believer in the eight steps, incorporating these components into your current customer satisfaction measurement process will pinpoint your strengths and identify opportunities for improvement.

Survey Questions

Please evaluate the following statements on a scale of 1 to 5; 5 is strongly agree, and 1 is strongly disagree. Any rating below a 5 suggests your company may be vulnerable to competition.

Step 1—Make me feel welcome

- Made me feel welcome

- Provided me with the level of service I was hoping for

Step 2—Give me your full attention

- Gave me their full attention

- Understood how I was feeling

Step 3—Answer more than my question

- Conversation was personalized to my situation

- Provided me with additional information

Step 4—Know your stuff

- Trusted that I was given an accurate response

- Knowledgeable about the company's products, services, and policies

Step 5—Don't tell me no

- Interaction/transaction took little effort on my part

- Told me what they could do, not what they couldn't do

Step 6—Invite me to return

- Made me feel they wanted to see or hear from me again

- Made me feel my business was appreciated

Step 7—Show me I matter

- Continued to communicate with me after the interaction/ transaction

- Interested in my continued satisfaction with the product or service

Step 8—Surprise me in good ways **

- Made me feel like I am a special and important customer

- Surprised me in some way after the interaction/transaction

Creating your Repeat Business Scorecard: TCFCR determines the Repeat Business Scorecard by calculating the percentage of "5" ratings for each survey attribute. For instance, if 70 percent of the customers gave your company a "5" for "made me feel welcome" and 60 percent a "5" for "provided the level of service I was hoping for," your combined score would be 65 percent (70% + 60% = 130% divided by 2 = 65%) for Step 1 - Make Me Feel Welcome.

**Not all customers should be asked to evaluate the last element, "surprise me in good ways." Most companies experience the Pareto principle, also known as the 80-20 rule, where 80 percent of their business comes from 20 percent of their customers. As a general rule, the last element should be measured by the 20 percent.

Appendix II
Thought-Provoking Questions

Below are a series of questions, the answers to which are another vehicle for your company to gauge its journey to secure a higher percentage of repeat business. Use these thought-provoking questions to stimulate internal discussion about your customers and your company's relationship with them. You have read about the eight steps in *The Endangered Customer*; each one is unique and self-contained, but all should be followed to create an exemplary customer experience. The steps are sequential and point in a direction and ultimate destination. See where your company stands on the path, where your strengths lie, and where improvements can be made. If you focus on examining each step, it should be a fun and compelling exercise garnering amazing results along the way.

1. Do we have a policy of "person first, customer second?" How do we welcome customers when they first arrive at our store, call us, or visit our website? Do we replicate our welcoming and engaging approach on all channels, including social media?

2. Do we engage our customers on social media? Do we create solutions or only respond to inquires, complaints, or praise? How long does it take for us to respond?

3. Does our business culture and philosophy encourage relationship building, or do we rely solely on our brand image?

4. Do we have a policy for associates to give first-time customers special attention? Do associates always tell the customer their name and ask for the customer's name as well? Do we include this special attention on every communication channel: website, phone, e-mail, chat?

5. Do we train our associates to be observant and listen? Do associates understand the importance of creating a dialogue as a beginning to build a relationship?

6. Do we offer help to our customers: water on a hot day or a plastic bag for a wet umbrella?

7. Does every associate have a business card with his or her hours and contact information? Does every associate tell customers store hours, how to access the website, return policies, or other additional useful information that is helpful? Do we encourage customers to join in social media?

8. Is it easy to find our telephone number, "Contact us" page, or hours of operation on our website?

9. Do our associates thank customers for shopping? Do we tell customers they are appreciated and valued? Do we give customers additional information to assist them, like hours of operation, best place to park, etc.? Do we include additional information across all channels of communication?

10. Does our company have rules about cell phones and if/when they can be used?

11. Are there procedures and training to ensure that customers feel like they are receiving an associate's undivided attention? Is there training provided to associates to encourage "active listening" so they not only hear what the customer is saying or asking but also understand how the customer is feeling?

12. Does every associate participate in continuing training about products and services? Are associates knowledgeable about products and services to develop trust with the customer?

13. What are our company's hiring practices? Is there high associate turnover? Are associates valued and treated with respect?

14. Does our company know which employees are providing personalized service? Is there a forum in place for associates to share their experiences and learn from each other?

15. Are associates asked their thoughts about how to improve service? Are their ideas and suggestions documented and implemented? Are associates thanked for their contributions?

16. If an associate wants to leave, does our company determine his or her true ROI to make a counteroffer?

17. Does our company obtain feedback from customers? Is the feedback based on different channels of commerce? Are the results what we were expecting? Do we implement change based on the acquired data?

18. Is it our company policy for associates to never say no without asking a supervisor or manager? Do associates respond to the customer in a timely manner?

19. How do associates show customers they matter and are important after a transaction is complete? Is it part of our company culture to tell customers we want to see or hear from them again? Do associates ask customers their preferences for future communication: phone, e-mail, or text?

20. How does our company use technology to enhance the customer experience? Do we have CRM systems to maintain customers' histories and use that to thank them? Do we know how often a customer does business with our company?

21. Does our business culture embrace the customer journey that begins with an initial transaction but should be continuous and never end? Do associates understand their crucial role in the customer experience? Do associates understand that a transaction is only one step in the customer journey?

22. Does our company reward and recognize our best customers? Do we know who they are? Do we surprise our customers in good ways? Have we explored how to provide that surprise to make our customers feel special and important?

23. Does our company measure our percentage of repeat business? What mechanism do we use? Do we segment the measurement or look only at year-to-year sales? Do we use the feedback to implement change?

Appendix III
The Center For Client Retention

The Center For Client Retention (TCFCR) was founded by Richard Shapiro in 1988 and provides customized research, training and consulting. TCFCR deep dives into a company's procedures, practices and communications determining strengths and weaknesses to create an exceptional customer experience, nurture loyalty and increase customer retention. TCFCR designs and conducts research, employee engagement surveys, mystery shopper (calls, emails, chats), competitive landscape benchmarking studies, and repeat business boot camps for companies to increase their percentage of repeat customers.

Richard's new book, *The Endangered Customer: Eight Steps to Guarantee Repeat Business*, is based on research compiled during TCFCR's 27-year history partnering with Fortune 500 corporations and small companies. The Repeat Business Risk Assessment (RBRA) measures the customer experience evaluating a company's policies, technology and communication materials using the eight steps. This comprehensive program in combination with TCFCR's Repeat Business Scorecard (RBS) enables any business entity to assess their at-risk retention factor with customers.

Competition is fierce between the global economy, connectivity, start-ups and third party sellers. The cost to acquire new customers is, as always, high and social media has impacted consumer shopping patterns, acquisition of customers and how companies conduct business. TCFCR's consulting and training can dramatically reduce any company's vulnerability to lost customers and help restructure corporate cultures to improve customer retention and create a unique, personalized customer experience for every buying channel in any industry.

For information about TCFCR's services including workshops, boot camps and keynotes, contact TCFCR at *info@tcfcr.com* or call 973-258-9400.

Endnotes

1. "Customer 2020: Are You Future-Ready or Reliving the Past?" Accenture report. https://www.accenture.com/ t00010101T000000__w__/it-it/_acnmedia/Accenture/ Conversion-Assets/DotCom/Documents/Local/it-it/PDF_3/ Accenture-Customer-2020-Future-Ready-Reliving-Past.pdf.

2. "The $6 Trillion Opportunity." Accenture report. https:// www.accenture.com/us-en/insight-digital-improve-customer-experience.aspx.

3. "American Express Global Customer Service Barometer." http:// about.americanexpress.com/news/docs/2014x/2014-Global-Customer-Service-Barometer-US.pdf.

4. "The $6 Trillion Opportunity." Ibid.

5. "Accenture 2013 Global Consumer Pulse Survey." http://www. accenture.com/sitecollectiondocuments/pdf/accenture-global-consumer-pulse-research-study-2013-key-findings.pdf.

6. "The CIO's and CMO's Blueprint for Strategy in the Age of the Customer." Forrester Research Report. April 2015. http://solutions. forrester.com/age-of-the-customer/cio-cmo-strategy-3115Q-3763IK.html.

7. "Online Extra: Jeff Bezos on Word-of-Mouth Power." *Bloomberg Businessweek,* Aug. 1, 2004. http://www.bloomberg.com/bw/ stories/2004-08-01/online-extra-jeff-bezos-on-word-of-mouth-power.

8. "Bazaarvoice and the Center for Generational Kinetics Release New Study on How Millennials Shop." News release. January 30, 2012. http://investors.bazaarvoice.com/releasedetail. cfm?releaseid=649677.

9. Piotr Winkelman and Kent C. Berridge. "Unconscious Emotion." *Current Directions in Psychological Science*, 2004. Pages 120–123.

10. Roger Dooley. "Smiles Really Do Boost Sales." Neuromarketing blog. October 27, 2007. http://www.neurosciencemarketing.com/ blog/articles/smiles-boost-sales.htm#sthash.RkQ1gcq9.dpuf.

11. "HBR Service with a Very Big Smile." https://hbr.org/2007/05/ service-with-a-very-big-smile.

12. Jason Fried. "Why I'm Sick of Slick Design." *Inc.*, April 2014. http:// www.inc.com/magazine/201404/jason-fried/do-not-overdesign-your-website.html

13. "Police Stress Deterrence Measures as Bank Robberies Surge in the City." *New York Times*, March 14, 2009.

14. Roben Farzad. "A Guerrilla Stock Analyst Plays Mystery Shopper at Sears." *Bloomberg BusinessWeek*, January 30, 2014.

15. Joanna Ellis. "Resident Retention: The Difference between Customer Satisfaction and Customer Loyalty." *Property Management Insider*, January 22, 2003. http://www.propertymanagementinsider.com/resident-retention-customer-loyalty.

16. M. Ellen Peebles. "Love Your Customers." *Harvard Business Review*, July–August 2006. https://hbr.org/2006/07/love-your-customers.

17. Linda Adams. "Paying Attention." HR.com blog, June 13, 2006. http://www.gordontraining.com/free-workplace-articles/paying-attention/.

18. Matthew Dixon, Karen Freeman, and Nicholas Toman. "Stop Trying to Delight Your Customers." Harvard Business Review, July-August 2010.

19. Richard B. Chase and Sriram Dasu. "Want to Perfect Your Company's Service? Use Behavioral Science." *Harvard Business Review*, June 2001. https://hbr.org/2001/06/want-to-perfect-your-companys-service-use-behavioral-science.

20. Nathan Lustig. "What I Learned from Laurie Benson." November 21, 2012. http://www.nathanlustig.com/2012/11/21/what-i-learned-from-laurie-benson/,

21. "Gartner Identifies the Top 10 Strategic Technology Trends for 2015." October 8, 2014. http://www.gartner.com/newsroom/id/2867917.

22. Jim Roddy. "Customer Experience Secrets of Brick-and-Mortar Superstars." *Integrated Solutions for Retailers*, January 13, 2014. http://www.innovativeretailtechnologies.com/doc/customer-experience-secrets-of-brick-and-mortar-superstars-0001.

23. "50 Facts about Customer Experience." *Return on Behavior Magazine*, October 2010. http://returnonbehavior.com/2010/10/50-facts-about-customer-experience-for-2011/.

24. Todd and Mike Shumaker of Confidential On-Site Paper Shredding

25. Thomas O. Jones and W. Earl Sasser Jr. "Why Satisfied Customers Defect." *Harvard Business Review,* November–December 1995. https://hbr.org/1995/11/why-satisfied-customers-defect.

26. Ibid.

27. Thomas H. Davenport et al. "Know What Your Customers Want Before They Do." *Harvard Business Review*, December 2011. https://hbr.org/2011/12/know-what-your-customers-want-before-they-do.

28. "Bazaarvoice and the Center for Generational Kinetics Release New Study on How Millennials Shop." News release, January 30, 2012. http://investors.bazaarvoice.com/releasedetail.cfm?releaseid=649677.

29. Guillermo Valiente. "Building Collaborative Relationships with Millennials." *Business2Community*, April 20, 2013. http://www.business2community.com/customer-experience/building-collaborative-relationships-with-millennials-0471067.

30. "Millennials: Breaking the Myths." Nielsen Holdings, N.V., January 27, 2014. Full report at http://digitalmarketingstrategiessummit. com/assets/files/presentations/Mancini_Report.pdf.

31. "Human Relationships Are All That Matter in Customer Experience." The Customer Edge blog, October 22, 2013. http:// scn.sap.com/community/customer-edge/blog/2013/10/22/ human-relationships-are-all-that-matter-in-customer-experience.

32. Carmine Gallo. "BMW Radically Rethinks the Car Buying Experience." *Forbes*, April 18, 2014. http://www.forbes.com/sites/ carminegallo/2014/04/18/bmw-radically-rethinks-the-car-buying- experience/.

33. "BMW Dealers with Product Geniuses Boost Profit and Customer Satisfaction." *Europe Auto News*, April, 2014. http://europe. autonews.com/article/20140417/ANE/140419860/bmw-dealers- with-product-geniuses-boost-profit-and-customer.

34. Francoise Carré, Chris Tilly, and Diana Denham. "Explaining Variation in the Quality of US Retail Jobs." Annual Meeting of the Labor and Employment Relations Association, Denver, CO, January 2010.

35. "Container Store Bets on $50,000 Retail Worker." *Wall Street Journal*, October 14, 2014. http://www.wsj.com/articles/ container-store-bets-on-50-000-retail-worker-1413340639.

36. "Paying Employees to Stay, Not to Go." *New York Times*, July 4, 2014. http://www.nytimes.com/2014/07/05/business/economy/ boloco-and-shake-shack-offer-above-average-pay.html.

37. "The World's Greatest Stock Picker? Bet You Sold Apple and Google a Long Time Ago." *Washington Post,* October 14, 2014. http://www.washingtonpost.com/business/even-if-you-could-pick-huge-winners-could-you-hold-them/2014/10/03/bd426e34-49ba-11e4-891d-713f052086a0_story.html.

38. "Shake Shack IPO Prices Far above Expected Range." *Wall Street Journal*, January 29, 2015. http://www.reuters.com/article/2015/01/29/us-shake-shack-ipo-report-idUSKBN0L22VZ20150129.

39. "Henry Ford Didn't Pay $5 a Day Just to Be Nice." *Newsday,* December 13, 2013. http://www.newsday.com/opinion/columnists/lane-filler/henry-ford-didn-t-pay-5-a-day-just-to-be-nice-lane-filler-1.6629767.

40. "Job Hunting in the Network Age." *Wall Street Journal*, July 18, 2014. http://www.wsj.com/articles/the-weekend-interview-job-hunting-in-the-network-age-1405724333.

41. "Paying Employees to Stay, Not to Go." *New York Times*, July 4, 2014. http://www.nytimes.com/2014/07/05/business/economy/boloco-and-shake-shack-offer-above-average-pay.html.

42. Meghan M. Biro. "Happy Employees = Hefty Profits." *Forbes.com*, January 19, 2014. http://www.forbes.com/sites/meghanbiro/2014/01/19/happy-employees-hefty-profits/.

43. "Flyin' a Family Business with Radio Flyer." *Fortune*, May 2014. http://fortune.com/2014/05/01/flyin-a-family-business-with-radio-flyer/.

44. "What to Do When You Can't Say Yes." Shep Hyken blog. http://www.hyken.com/customer-service-3/1116-2/.

45. Lewis Schiff. *Business Brilliant* (New York: Harper Business, 2013), 153.

46. "What's the Best Thing a Customer Ever Said to You?" 1 to 1 Media, *Introducing the 2011 Customer Service Champs.* http://www.1to1media.com/downloads/2011ChampsBook.pdf.

47. "The Secret to Airbnb's Freakishly Rapid Orgy Response." *Fast Company*, March 17, 2014. http://www.fastcompany.com/3027798/the-secret-to-airbnbs-freakishly-rapid-orgy-response-scenario-planning?partner.

48. "2013 Customer Rage Study." CCMC. http://www.customercaremc.com/wp/wp-content/uploads/2014/01/KeyFindingsFrom2013NationalCustomerRageSurvey.pdf.

49. "McCormick CEO Helps Find 5-Year-Old Customer's Favorite, but Discontinued, Spice." *Baltimore Sun,* December 1, 2013. http://articles.baltimoresun.com/2013-12-01/business/bs-bz-mccormick-spice-ceo-20131127_1_ceo-tim-cook-spice-macbook-pro.

50. "Broken Guitar Has United Playing the Blues to the Tune of $180 Million." *Fast Company*, July 30, 2009. http://www.fastcompany.com/1320152/broken-guitar-has-united-playing-blues-tune-180-million.

51. Dave Carroll. *United Breaks Guitars: The Power of One Voice in the Age of Social Media* (Hay House 2013).

52. "Returning to Wal-Mart: Human Cashiers." *Wall Street Journal,* August 15, 2014. http://www.wsj.com/articles/wal-mart-pledges-to-staff-checkout-lanes-during-holidays-1408112765.

53. M. Ellen Peebles. "Love Your Customers." *Harvard Business Review*, July-August 2006. https://hbr.org/2006/07/love-your-customers.

54. "Science Explains Why Surprise Brings Us Pleasure." Fusion.net, April 1, 2015. http://fusion.net/story/112615/why-surprise-is-so-good-for-your-brain-and-body/.

55. "Customers Will Be Loyal If Delight Is Built into Your Product or Service." *Entrepreneur*, May 11, 2015. http://www.entrepreneur.com/article/245961

56. "Dr. Wael Asaad, Brown University. Surprise and Memory Formation," interview on WAMC-FM. http://wamc.org/post/dr-wael-asaad-brown-university-surprise-and-memory-formation#stream/0.

57. Scott Redick. "Surprise Is Still the Most Powerful Marketing Tool." *Harvard Business Review*, May 10, 2013. https://hbr.org/2013/05/surprise-is-still-the-most-powerful/.

58. Richard B. Chase and Sriram Dasu. "Want to Perfect Your Company's Service? Use Behavioral Science." *Harvard Business Review*, June 2001. https://hbr.org/2001/06/want-to-perfect-your-companys-service-use-behavioral-science.

59. "The Secret to Secret's Success? BPA." *Advertising Age*, February 14, 2011. http://adage.com/article/digital/social-media-secret-deodorant-s-random-acts-kindness/148829/.

60. "GQ Cover: Lands' End Customers Freak Out Over 'Pornographic' Photo." *Hollywood Life*, August 15, 2014. http://hollywoodlife.com/2014/08/15/lands-end-gq-magazine-emily-ratajkowski/.

Acknowledgments

THE ENDANGERED CUSTOMER: Eight Steps
to Guarantee Repeat Business could not have been written without
the help of numerous friends, colleagues, clients, and family. I would
especially like to extend my profound thanks and appreciation to the
following people who provided significant contributions to this, my second book.

Noel Weyrich, *my editor and collaborator*
Susi Weiner, *my best friend and partner*
Dawn Kirspel, *my colleague, friend, and vice president, The Center For
Client Retention*

I want to thank some very special Welcomers who know and understand that the customer experience begins with the first encounter and
never ends:

Suzan Campbell, loves providing and sharing additional information
Iron Copelev, teaches us all about "inviting to return"
Jefferson Cuevas, understands the concept of "pay it forward"
Lynn Krohn, connects instantly
Robin Kettler, shows her customers they matter

Wayne Mize, gives you his complete attention

Rochelle Perlman, knows her customers as well as she knows her merchandise

Lynne Schwartz, surprises in good ways

Michael Tehrani, always offers two solutions

Javier Yepez, makes everyone feel welcome

I would like to thank the following for endorsing my first book and encouraging me to write a second:

Chip Conley

Chip R. Bell

Frederic Fekkai

Shep Hyken

Robert Spector

My new friends who have been highly supportive of my thought-leadership:

Greg Furman, founder and chairman, The Luxury Marketing Council

Mike Greece, managing partner, The Pollack Group

Jack Killion, partner, Eagle Rock Partners & Bluestone+Killion

Chad McDaniel, founder and president, Execs in the Know

Jack Mitchell, chairman, Mitchell Family of Stores

Paul Squires, owner, AS & K

Lastly, always thankful for my immediate and extended family, with special love for my first grandchild, Sarah Harper Shapiro.